Does God Exist?

Does God Exist?

A Socratic Dialogue on
the Five Ways of Thomas Aquinas

Matt Fradd & Robert A. Delfino

 ENROUTE

En Route Books & Media

5705 Rhodes Avenue, St. Louis, MO 63109

Contact us at contactus@enroutebooksandmedia.com

Cover design by T.J. Burdick

Cover painting by Joos van Gent (fl.1460-75) and Pedro Berruguete (c.1450-1504)

Paperback ISBN: 978-0-9996670-7-1

E-book ISBN: 978-0-9996670-9-5

Printed in the United States of America

1 3 5 7 9 10 8 6 4 2

TOTUS TUUS MARIA

Contents

Acknowledgements

I am very grateful for the following people who, whether they know it or not, have helped me gain a better understanding of the teachings of St. Thomas Aquinas and the arguments for the existence of God. In particular, I'm grateful for the work of Trent Horn, Edward Feser, Peter Kreeft, William Lane Craig, D.Q. McInerny, Jimmy Akin, Karlo Broussard, Bishop Scott McCaig, Bishop Robert Barron, and of course, my co-author, Robert Delfino, who not only helped me to write this book but also taught me a lot about Thomistic metaphysics in the process. I am also grateful to Sebastian Mahfood, who agreed to let us write this book for En Route Books and Media, and to Cynthia Gniadek, who not only edited this manuscript but helped refine it. I am thankful for my wife, Cameron, who patiently (oh, so patiently) helped me during the writing process and is always a source of insight and inspiration. Above all, I'm thankful to Almighty God for His grace and for allowing me to write poorly of Him (It's the only way anyone can write of Him, though there are degrees; I'm on the lower end).

—*Matt Fradd*

I have been blessed by God with wonderful family members, teachers, colleagues, and friends. To my mother and father, Anita and Anthony, I owe a great debt—their love and encouragement made all the difference. I have also been sustained by the love of my wife, Marialena, and my sons, Jonathan and Erik, who give me joy. Among my philosophy teachers, I am grateful to Richard Ingardia, who introduced me to Thomas Aquinas, and to Peter A. Redpath and Jorge J. E. Gracia, who helped shape my understanding of the Angelic Doctor. I'm also indebted to Joseph Owens, Armand Maurer, John F. Wippel, John F. X. Knasas, and W. Norris Clarke, whose work I have found invaluable. My department at St. John's University, NY, has always been supportive, especially Paul Gaffney, Art Gianelli, Glenn Statile, Marie George, and Alice Ramos. Other colleagues and friends of mine have endured discussions with me about Aquinas and metaphysics, often giving useful feedback, including William Byrne, Rachel Hollander, Robert Fanuzzi, Chiara and Brian Lockey, Miguel Roig, Philip Drucker, Roberta Hayes, Peter Albano, David Kaspar, Mark Kiley, David Haddorff, Joan Ball, Tom and Lillian Riley, Jerome Hillock, Al and Becky Tantala, Jonathan Bricklin, David Shear, Penny Goldstein, and Amanda DeLalla. I received helpful comments on early drafts of chapters from Stephen Greeley, Andrew Gniadek, Erin Gawera, Rick Barrett, Lara Thompson, and Kristen Fusaro-Pizzo. To Matt Fradd and Sebastian Mahfood, OP, who invited me to be part of the life of this book, I am extremely grateful. Finally, none of this would have been possible without the love and help I have received from God. It is an honor to be called to speak of Him who has given me everything, and to whom I can give nothing but my love.

—*Robert A. Delfino*

Preface

Matt Fradd

When I grew up, I had a lot of questions about God, the meaning of life, and what happens after death. "How do we know God exists?" I wondered. I didn't see Him, feel Him, or hear Him. At the time, the word "atheist" was not a shorthand way of saying, "I'm more intelligent than you," as it apparently is today—if it were, I probably would have said I was one. At the time I said, and rightly so, that I was "agnostic." I didn't know if God existed, and I didn't want to believe or base my life on Him just because my parents or grandparents did. I wanted to believe in His existence only if it were true. And so I asked a lot of questions: Why does God let bad things happen to good people? Who created God? Aren't all religions, deep down, saying the same thing?

Whenever I brought these questions to a priest, to family, or to friends, the questions were usually met with one simple reply: "It's a mystery." In response to what seemed like a dismissive answer, I always thought to myself, "Ah...well, maybe it is, but could you at least give it a shot?!?" My faith was waning, and there seemed to be little hope for recovery. What I needed were answers. What I needed was someone who could explain those answers. What I needed was someone like...well...St. Thomas.

I wish I had known then what I know now about St. Thomas Aquinas and his writings on the existence of God. By the age of thirteen, I had decided that God probably doesn't exist and that religion is something people follow to make themselves feel good. Praying, to me, was like keeping a journal or talking to a therapist—you feel better because you get your feelings out, not because you are corresponding with some metaphysical dude up in the clouds (the fact that I viewed God as a "dude" is, again, evidence that someone should have hit me with a volume of the *Summa* . . . and then explained it to me).

The truth, I later learned, is that Catholicism is both a sensual and an intellectual religion. The First Vatican Council proclaimed that we can know God exists completely apart from divine revelation.[1] In other words, we can come to believe in God's existence just by using our natural human reason to draw conclusions about what we observe in the world around us. Not only is it reasonable to believe in the existence of God, but it's also reasonable to believe in those mysteries that are divinely revealed and continuously proclaimed in the Catholic Tradition. I was 17 years old when I came to believe in Christ (I'm 33 now), and the more I grow in my Catholic faith, the more I see just how reasonable it is. I want you to see how reasonable the faith is too, but more fundamentally, I want you to see how reasonable belief in God's existence is. For this reason, I decided to write a book to share with you the reasons for God's existence that St. Thomas Aquinas outlined in his *Summa theologiae*. Along the way, I met Robert Delfino, a philosophy professor who specializes in Aquinas and who was very excited about an early draft of this book. He offered some suggestions, and after a few conversations, it became apparent that if this book was going to be a thorough and faithful presentation of Thomas's five ways, he would need do more than offer suggestions; he would need to write it with me.

Let me close by sharing one more story with you. I mentioned earlier that I was 17 when I came to believe in Christ, but I did not tell you how. When I was 17, my mother sent me to World Youth Day in Rome. I looked forward to it because it was a free trip to Italy, but I never imagined how it would change my life. It was there that I returned to faith in Christ. And do you know what I saw there that changed me? For the first time in my life, I met faithful Catholics who were reasonable! All of those questions I had as a child were finally coming to light. Any frustrations I had from the dismissive "It's a mystery" answer were relieved. This encounter with faithful, reasonable Catholics led me to a deeper, more personal encounter with God. Since that time, I have continued to grow in my faith, always being supported by an increased knowledge of rational arguments for God's existence, such as those given by Aquinas.

When I went to World Youth Day, I got to see Pope John Paul II. He was an inspiration to me then, and he continues to be now. Among his many writings, I have found myself continually drawn to a statement he made in his encyclical *Fides et ratio*—a statement that describes my struggle and return to the faith, my inspiration for writing this book, and my hope for what you will see in the dialogue contained in this book. The statement is this: "Faith and reason are like two wings on which the human spirit rises to the contemplation of truth; and God has placed in the human heart a desire to know the truth."[2] Within this book, you will find a dialogue that simplifies the five arguments St. Thomas Aquinas has for the existence of God. It is our prayer that this book sheds light on how God is the only explanation for the existence of reality and, in turn, helps lead you to faith or deepens your understanding of it.

Introduction

Aquinas discusses five ways that people can come to know that God exists.[3] He calls these five ways "demonstrations" (proofs), and he discusses them in many of his works.[4] However, it is his concise versions in the *Summa theologiae* (Summary of theology), which were intended for beginning students of theology, that most people encounter. Unfortunately, because they were written over seven centuries ago in a pre-modern philosophical and theological language, many modern readers have difficulty understanding them.

In this book we make learning the five ways fun and easy by explaining them through a dialogue between AJ and Lucy—two characters with whom you will quickly become familiar and relate. AJ and Lucy share insight and humor as AJ offers two objections to theism and then explores Aquinas's five proofs, which Lucy presents as a challenge to AJ's atheistic beliefs.

As the story unfolds, the key terms and concepts you need to understand the five ways of Aquinas will be explained as needed. Through different examples and analogies, and by raising and answering objections along the way, you will gain an understanding of these important terms and concepts.

1

However, in case you want more help or want to dive deeper in your understanding of Aquinas, we have also included other resources in Part II of the book and in the endnotes.

Part II of the book begins with chapter ten, which explains in greater detail over a dozen terms and concepts, such as being and essence and the different kinds of causes that Aquinas discusses. In a way similar to a glossary, it is arranged according to section headings, so you can easily find what you're looking for. Chapter eleven is a synopsis of Lucy's versions of the five ways, which you should read after reading the main dialogue, as it will make much more sense then. Chapter twelve lists suggested reading material that you might find helpful in learning more about Aquinas and the arguments for and against the existence of God. Finally, the endnotes mostly supply citations to passages in Aquinas and other authors, should you desire to dig deeper into those works, while occasionally clarifying some of the more difficult points.

Now that you know how to take advantage of all the resources in this book, you are ready to enter the dialogue and meet the characters, Lucy and AJ.

***

In order to get this book into more hands, we'd like to invite you to help us spread the word. If you take a photo of yourself with this book and share it on Twitter or Instagram with the hashtag "#5Ways", we will give you free access to an hour-long interview we (Matt and Robert) had about the origin of this book and why we're so excited about it, and we'll let you ask us, the authors, one question about the content you'll find in this book.

Part I

THE DIALOGUE

Chapter 1
An Atheist and a Christian Walk Into a Coffee Shop

Lucy: "I'm an atheist, debate me?" Wow…that sure is a cute, confrontational shirt you got there…

AJ: Yeah, got it online. Glad you like it.

Lucy: I'm Lucy.

AJ: AJ…. *And* now I feel awkward 'cause you're reading the, uh…

Lucy: The Bible? Yep.

AJ: Mind if I join you?

Lucy: Hmm, I'm a bit hesitant, but okay.

AJ: Thanks. Look what *I'm* here to read!

Lucy: Wow! Dawkins. *The God Delusion*. How original of you.

AJ: I could say the same about you—the Bible?

Lucy: Touché…. Is this the part where you get all confrontational?

AJ: Maybe. Dawkins says …

Lucy: I've read it.

AJ: Really?

Lucy: Really.

AJ: Do you remember what he said about the God of the Old Testament?

Lucy: Yeah, I do, but go ahead, refresh my memory.

AJ: "The God of the Old Testament is arguably the most unpleasant character in all fiction: jealous and proud of it; a petty, unjust, unforgiving control-freak; a vindictive, bloodthirsty ethnic cleanser; a misogynistic, homophobic, racist, infanticidal, genocidal, filicidal, pestilential, megalomaniacal, sadomasochistic, capriciously malevolent bully."[5]

Lucy: It's well written, for sure. His book as a whole, however, I found disappointing. I hope you're not wearing that shirt because of Dawkins. Why are you an atheist anyway?

AJ: Well, partly because…Let's see here…"The God of the Old Testament is arguably the most unpleasant …"

Lucy: I get it, I get it.

AJ: You asked.

Lucy: How does that follow though?

AJ: How does what follow?

Lucy: "This religion's account of God is horrid; therefore, God does not exist."

AJ: It's not just that it's horrid; it's that it's contradictory. In the Old Testament he's a malevolent bully; in the New Testament he's a peace-loving hippie.

Lucy: Well, as formidable as your Biblical interpretation skills are, so what?

Let's say you're right. Maybe the Bible is false.

AJ: I'm glad we agree…. My Latte's ready. One sec.

***

AJ: Sorry about that. Continue.

Lucy: Seriously? The great atheist debater said yes to sprinkles?

AJ: Hey! Sprinkles are awesome, okay! So, what were you saying?

Lucy: I was saying maybe the Bible is false. Obviously I don't think that, but let's suppose I'm wrong. How would that prove God doesn't exist?

AJ: It's not just the Bible; every formulation of God's existence from every religion I've studied—and I've studied a lot!—amounts to nothing more than anthropomorphic twaddle.

Lucy: Okay. Let's say you're right. I still don't think that's a good reason to think God does not exist. That would be like me saying, "I've studied the history of alien abductions. I have interviewed every living claimant and have found all their stories to be bogus. Therefore, aliens do not exist." Do you see how that's a logical fallacy? The conclusion doesn't follow the premises.

AJ: I think it's important to remember, Lucy, that you're the one who has the burden of proof here. You're the one who claims God exists.

Lucy: I agree I have a burden of proof, but so do you, unless you're not an atheist after all!

AJ: This is a common misconception. An atheist isn't one who says God does not exist; an atheist just lacks belief in the God you claim does exist. And all gods for that matter.

Lucy: Don't take this the wrong way, but I'm not actually interested in what you believe.

AJ: Ouch? …

Lucy: What I mean is, if you're going to redefine atheism to mean a "lack of belief," then what you're doing is trivializing what has traditionally been meant by "atheism." This definition of yours would make atheism not a claim to knowledge, but merely a state of mind. And I'm not interested in your state of mind; I'm interested in what's true.

AJ: It's not a redefinition. That's what we've always meant by it.

Lucy: See, I know enough to know that that isn't true. I'm in the process of getting my master's degree in philosophy, and one of the standard encyclopedias of philosophy we use is the *Routledge Encyclopedia of Philosophy*.

AJ: You *literally* just pulled out an encyclopedia from your bag.

Lucy: Like I said, I study philosophy. Here's what it says: "Atheism is the position that affirms the non-existence of God. It proposes positive disbelief rather than mere suspension of belief."[6] What you're talking about is agnosticism, from the Greek word *agnostos*, meaning "without knowledge."

AJ: Look, I think that if I've made the sincere effort to discover the truth about something and have found all the evidence in favor of that thing lacking, then I'm justified in saying that that thing doesn't exist. Besides, you're an atheist with regards to every other god humanity has postulated. I just go one step further. I'm consistent.

Lucy: Okay, two points. Let me address the "you're an atheist about other gods" one first. You're right, I don't believe in Zeus, Thor, Horus, or any other pagan god. But that doesn't make me an atheist. An atheist is someone who doesn't believe in God. I do believe in God; therefore, I'm not an atheist. Let me give you an analogy. Do you think that monarchy is a good form of government?

AJ: No.

Lucy: What about a kakistocracy, where the government is led by the least qualified to govern? Do you think that is a good form of government?

AJ: Hmm. I thought that was what we were in now, no? No, I don't think that's a good form of government; what's your point?

Lucy: My point is, I'm no more an atheist because I reject some versions of god than you are an anarchist because you reject some forms of government.[7] Now on to your first point about having made a good effort to see if a thing is true. Now we're going 'round in circles. Remember what I said about the aliens? Suppose I make a sincere effort to discover the truth about extraterrestrial life and find all the evidence in favor of it lacking. That doesn't warrant the conclusion that aliens don't exist. They may still exist even though we have no good evidence to think they do.

AJ: So you're saying God's an alien?

Lucy: No, I'm saying God may exist even if you think there are no good reasons to believe.

AJ: What reasons do you have to think God exists?

Lucy: Wait a minute. Before we get to that, we need to finish defining our terms. Have you read Trent Horn's book *Answering Atheism*?[8] If not, you need to read it. He says there are three ways a person can respond to the question, does God exist?—yes, no, or maybe. It therefore makes the most sense that we have three terms. If you say yes, you're a theist; if you say no, you're an atheist; and if you say maybe, you're an agnostic. And if you do say no, as you have done, then you're making a claim to knowledge that you need to give reasons for. Even one will do. So…what is your reason?

Chapter 2

The Problem of Evil

AJ: There's no one reason. I just see no reason to think he *does* exist.... You look disappointed.

Lucy: Kind of, yeah. How would you respond if I said about my belief in God, "There's no one reason. I just, well…I see no reason to think atheism is true."

AJ: Fair enough. Well, how about the problem of evil? Right now, as we sit here drinking coffee in these cushy chairs, people are starving to death, and children are being sexually trafficked. Think about that for a moment. Right now. That doesn't bother you!?

Lucy: Of course it bothers me!

AJ: How could a loving God allow that?

Lucy: Well, I do think the problem of evil is the greatest emotional obstacle to belief in God. But while I think it's a strong emotional obstacle, I don't think it's a strong intellectual one. Let me show you what I mean. Some Christians might say to you something like, "How can you say that your deceased loved ones are no more! How horrible to believe that you'll never see them again." That's a strong emotional obstacle to atheism, perhaps; but you, at least, don't think it's a good intellectual argument, right?

AJ: Right, it's wish fulfillment, pure and simple. But the problem of evil isn't like that. I mean, I think it *is* a good argument against God. Look, the atheist philosopher J. L. Mackie—I'm sure you've heard of him—maintained that belief in God is irrational, for if God were all-knowing, he would know that there is evil in the world; and if he were all-powerful he could prevent it; and if he were all-good, then he would wish to prevent it. The fact that there is still evil in the world proves that your God doesn't exist, or if he does, that he must be "impotent, ignorant, or wicked."[9] What do you think about that?

Lucy: Yes, I'm aware of Mackie's argument. I don't think it works.

AJ: Why?

Lucy: Mackie was wrong: the existence of God and the existence of evil aren't mutually exclusive.[10] How about we take a look at the three attributes he mentions—omnipotence, omniscience, and omnibenevolence?

AJ: Yeah. Start with his omnipotence. Why isn't your God strong enough to prevent evil?

Lucy: Omnipotence doesn't mean the ability to do what is logically impossible.[11]

AJ: Why not?

Lucy: Why not? What do you mean, why not?

AJ: If God is all-powerful, why can't he do the logically impossible?

Lucy: Because what is logically impossible is contradictory; and what is contradictory cannot exist in reality. In a contradiction, one part negates the other. God can't create a square circle, because to be circular is not to be square and vice versa. No object in reality can be both square and circular. God also can't lie—to do so would contradict his nature.

AJ: Can God create a rock too heavy for him to lift?

Lucy: Right, that's another example. This objection is essentially asking, can an all-powerful being create something that proves he's not all-powerful? But again, that's a contradiction. It's like saying God is both all-powerful and not all-powerful—but that's not possible. That phrase can't correspond to anything in reality. It borders on nonsense, AJ. The words have meaning but one part of the phrase negates the other. It's the kind of thing we can say out loud but when we think about it we realize it's impossible—or at least we should.

AJ: Okay, fair enough, but we're not talking about rocks or square circles; we're talking about evil. Why can't an all-powerful being prevent that?

Lucy: Right, I was getting to that. It's possible for God to create beings with the kind of free will that can choose between good and evil, yeah? But he can't also force those creatures to freely choose good. If he forced their choice, it wouldn't be free. There's a great quote from C.S. Lewis, who said, "If you choose to say, 'God can give a creature free will and at the same time withhold free will from it,' you have not succeeded in saying *anything* about God."[12] In other words, God isn't going to withhold free will after having given it. If, all things being equal, it's better that some creatures have free will than not, then we have to accept the possibility that evil may occur. Free creatures may commit moral evils. It reminds me of something

13

St. Augustine said: "[A] runaway horse is better than a stone that stays in the right place only because it has no movement or perception of its own; and in the same way, a creature that sins by free will is more excellent than one that does not sin only because it has no free will."[13]

AJ: Okay, well, let's say for the sake of argument that belief in God's existence isn't necessarily irrational. Isn't his existence still highly improbable in light of the meaningless suffering creatures have to endure?

Lucy: How do you know it's meaningless? I don't think it's meaningless in light of God's second attribute: his omniscience. If God has infinite knowledge, then he knows many things we don't, right? This means that he may, in fact, have good reasons for permitting things like evil and suffering, though they seem inexplicable to us. We human beings have a very limited vantage point, so we often lack knowledge about things of great significance. What appears to us to be a tragedy may actually be something that brings about great good, and conversely what appears to us as a good thing may, in the long run, prove harmful.

AJ: If God has good reasons to let us suffer, then why doesn't he at least let those who are suffering feel his presence? If I have a kid one day and he's suffering, you better believe I'll be by his side the entire time, telling him that I love him and am there for him.

Lucy: Well, as a Christian, that's precisely what I believe God has done and is doing. Not only does he console us through his revelation, the sacraments, and the help of others, he also entered into our suffering. He endured the most ignominious, torturous death imaginable to show his love for us. And so we can never say, "You don't know what I'm going through."

AJ: Well, I think the idea of a God who decides to have himself killed to show us he loves us is ridiculous, I have to say.

Lucy: Just because it appears ridiculous from *your* vantage point, AJ, doesn't mean it is ridiculous. Anyway, I'd like to get back to your analogy of the suffering child. I think that analogy actually makes my point. Think about a small child being taken to the doctor for his immunization shots. He knows the needle hurts, and he can't understand why his own parents are allowing the doctor to cause him pain. He doesn't understand that the inoculations help prevent the much greater suffering of disease. He's unable to perceive the greater good. In a similar way, we should recognize that a being with more knowledge than us, like God, may have good reasons for things, even pain and suffering, that we are unaware of. And so he allows evil to exist because of his omniscience, not in spite of it.

AJ: I can tell you've thought about this a lot, and I respect that, but I'm not buying it. I mean, what about God's third attribute—his omnibenevolence? God is supposed to be all-good and perfectly loving. What loving father allows his children to endure awful amounts of suffering if he could prevent it?

Lucy: Well, I think I've begun to address that by talking about what God's omnipotence does *not* mean, preventing people from using their free will to harm each other, and how God's omniscience means He may have good reasons for allowing us to suffer. Perhaps a big part of our problem is that we have this false, hallmark view of God. We think of God as the ... well, wait. Let me read something C.S. Lewis talked about in *The Problem of Pain* ... Just looking it up. Here it is:

> By the goodness of God we mean nowadays almost exclusively His lovingness; and in this we may be right. And by Love, in this context, most of us mean kindness…What would really satisfy us would be a God who said of anything we happened to like doing, "What does it matter so long as they are contented?" We want, in fact, not so much a Father in Heaven as a grand-father in heaven—a senile benevolence who, as they say, "liked to see young people enjoying themselves", and whose plan for the universe was simply that it might be truly said at the end of each day, "a good time was had by all."[14]

I think many people have this sort of view of God. And, look, if that's the sort of God Christians were saying exists, then I'd agree, he either doesn't exist or is doing a terrible job, but this isn't at all the God of Christianity. We don't believe that God created us merely for happiness in this life, but also, and most importantly, for eternal happiness with him in the next.

AJ: Are you telling me that if something tragic happened to you, it wouldn't shake your faith?

Lucy: No, I'm not saying that.

AJ: Well, what would it take?

Lucy: To lose my faith?

AJ: Yeah.

Lucy: I think a more interesting and fruitful question, for our purposes, is what *should* it take, not what *would* it take. I have no idea what would make me lose my faith. Maybe if I found out I had cancer or that my dad had died in a motorbike accident, that would do it. But this gets back to what I was saying earlier. The problem of evil can cause a strong emotional obstacle to belief in God—the evil of cancer or losing my dad might make me lose faith—but I don't think it *should*. Anyway, I don't think the problem of evil is a strong intellectual argument against the existence of God. In fact, rather than disproving God's existence, I think the reality of evil actually points to God's existence. If evil exists, then it follows that morality exists. If morality exists, then it follows that God exists.

AJ: I don't see how that follows at all…

Lucy: Okay, let me ask you this: what do you think evil is? How do you define it?

AJ: Hmm, I feel like we should have probably cleared that up earlier. Stuff that's not right—things we would never want to happen. How do you define it?

Lucy: I think I'd say evil is the way things should not be. When we think of school shootings, sexual trafficking, the stuff you mentioned earlier, we have this inherent reaction that it's not right, that these things shouldn't be happening.

AJ: Okay, yeah.

Lucy: But if there's a way things should not be, doesn't that imply that there's a way things should be? My point is simply that if atheism is true, there isn't a way things should be. There might be social norms, behavior that we as a society deem either acceptable or unacceptable, but there wouldn't be a way things *should* be. Since evil implies there is a way things should be, it sort of serves as an indirect proof against atheism, don't you think?

AJ: Why isn't there a way things should be if atheism is true?

Lucy: Because, if atheism is true things just are; and, as David Hume says, you can't derive an *ought* from an *is*—you can't argue how things *should be* from how they exist *now*.[15]

AJ: You're referring to Hume's Law, yes?

Lucy: Yes. Don't you see how if Hume's Law is true there can be no real evil because there is no way things should be? If Hume's Law is true, then evil is just an illusory psychological projection of ours on the world.

AJ: Wait a minute. If Hume's Law is true, then it is impossible to derive an ought from an is. But didn't you say earlier that God can't do the impossible?

Lucy: I did.

AJ: So, if Hume's law is true, then evil does not exist, as you said a moment ago. But if evil does not exist, then you can't argue, as you did earlier, that the reality of evil points to God's existence.

Lucy: Not bad, AJ. But I have a response.

AJ: I'm all ears.

Lucy: Well, it's not really mine. I got it from reading Alasdair MacIntyre's book *After Virtue*.[16] Let me see, I might have it in my bag …. Nope. Well, anyway, it basically boils down to this. God, as an intelligent and free cause, can endow things with natural functions and purposes. When something has a natural function, there are ways it should act and ways it should not act, and this lays the basis for morality. Only in such a moral framework can the sufferings of this life have any meaning. It may be a mystery why an all-good God allows suffering and evil to take place, but at least on this view there is meaning and purpose, and God can ultimately bring about justice and draw good out of the sufferings of this life.

AJ: So, it sounds like you're saying that Hume's Law is true if atheism is true, and false if theism is true—which means I've argued you into a stalemate.

Lucy: That's not how I see it. Earlier I said that the *reality* of evil actually points to God's existence because I thought you accepted the reality of evil.

AJ: Maybe I should have been clearer. It's not that I think evil literally exists, but that the goodness we should find if God exists is absent—and much of what we see seems so horrible. Let me read to you how Dawkins puts it. It's on my phone. One sec…okay, here it is:

> The total amount of suffering per year in the natural world is beyond all decent contemplation. During the minute that it takes me to compose this sentence, thousands of animals are being eaten alive; others are running for their lives, whimpering with fear; others are being slowly devoured from within by rasping parasites; thousands of all kinds are dying of starvation, thirst, and disease…. In a universe of blind physical forces and genetic replication, some people are going to get hurt, other people are going to get lucky, and you won't find any rhyme or reason in it, nor any justice. The universe we observe has precisely the properties we should expect if there is, at bottom, no design, no purpose, no evil and no good, nothing but blind, pitiless indifference.[17]

Lucy: Okay, that does help me understand better where you're coming from.

AJ: Good.

Lucy: Like I said earlier, the problem of evil is the greatest emotional obstacle to belief in God. It's also very complicated. We could probably talk about it for days, but I have to run now. I've got class in … shoot, ten minutes ago. It was nice meeting you, AJ.

AJ: Hey, you are not leaving because I was starting to win, are you?

Lucy: No, but I'm not surprised you'd say that!

AJ: Look, I don't want to hold you up, but do you come here often?

Lucy: Every morning. Religiously, you might say. Would you like to meet at the same time tomorrow and we can continue our discussion?

AJ: That'd be great. See you at 8?

Lucy: Sure. Talk to you then. God bless you, AJ.

Chapter 3

Is Science the Only Way to Know Truth?

Lucy: See, now that's a much more respectable shirt.

AJ: What can I say, our conversation yesterday really impacted me. I think you might be right about this whole Christianity thing.

Lucy: Seriously?

AJ: Nope.

Lucy: You're hysterical.

AJ: I do what I can … So yesterday you tried to show why my reasons for being an atheist aren't good, but do you have any positive reasons for thinking God exists? You do believe God's existence can be proven, right?

Lucy: It depends on what you mean by "prove," AJ. I don't think God's existence can be proven scientifically—for example, in physics or chemistry. But I do think that we can make a philosophical argument from things we observe about the world to a cause that strongly resembles the God of Christianity.

AJ: I feel like you're trying to get out of proving God by science.

Lucy: No, that's not what I'm trying to do.

AJ: Sounds like it to me.

Lucy: No, I'm saying that God's existence cannot in principle be proved by modern science. Let me give you two reasons why, okay?

AJ: I'm listening.

Lucy: Okay, the first reason—and I don't think you're going to like it—is that the scientific method of experimentation can't prove any theory definitively.

AJ: You're right, I don't like it. Plus, I think you're wrong. I mean, we've gained so much knowledge from science that I can't believe you just said that. Think of all the technology and life-saving medical procedures we have from science.

Lucy: AJ, I'm not anti-science. But when it comes to proof with a capital *P*, the scientific method does have limitations—and I'm not the first one to say this. The famous philosopher of science, Karl Popper, argued that a theory or statement "can never be finally established by establishing some of its consequences."[18]

AJ: You're going to have to do better than that—appeal to authority, really?

Lucy: Okay, let me give you a historical example that makes my point. Isaac Newton's theory of physics made predictions that were testable by scientific experiment. For about 250 years his theory passed all the experimental tests. I'm sure some people thought his theory had been proven true, but then Einstein came along. As objects approach the speed of light, Newton's theory no longer makes accurate predictions about their behavior, whereas Einstein's theory of relativity does. So, passing almost three centuries of tests was not enough to prove Newton's theory true. Scientific theories are always tentative because there's always a possibility that future evidence will show them to be flawed in some way.

AJ: Yeah, but even if Newton's theory wasn't totally true, there's still a lot of truth in it; otherwise, it wouldn't have made so many true predictions.

Lucy: I agree with you. It's inconceivable that Newton's theory could be totally false and yet make so many true predictions.[19] But while it's fair to say that Newton's theory *approximated* the truth, given certain parameters—that still falls short of proof in a strict sense.

AJ: You said you had two reasons why God's existence can't be proven by science. What's the other one?

Lucy: Simply, that the existence of God isn't a scientific question; it's a philosophical one. So, the scientific method isn't even appropriate in this case.

AJ: Why not? Dawkins says, "The existence of God is a scientific hypothesis like any other."[20]

Lucy: I know, but he's wrong.

AJ: Oh, well, in that case...

Lucy: Let me explain why. If the Christian understanding of God is correct, then God exists outside of space and time. But if that's true, then scientists can never study God directly. Do you think you can study something that exists outside of space and time in a laboratory?

AJ: Probably not.

Lucy: *Probably* not!?

AJ: Well, maybe they could come up with some clever experiments to detect God indirectly.

Lucy: I have doubts about that. But even if that were possible, lack of detection would not disprove God's existence—that was the point I made yesterday about aliens. Plus, there's another problem.

AJ: And what's that?

Lucy: Most scientists agree that science limits itself to the study of the natural world.[21] In other words, science has nothing to say about things *outside* the natural world. I'm not sure why you look so surprised. This is something recognized by both theists and atheists alike. Have you heard of the evolutionary biologist Steven Jay Gould?

AJ: I have. He's an atheist.

Lucy: Right. I have one of my favorite quotations from him on my phone. Here's what he says about all this:

> To say it for all my colleagues and for the umpteenth million time [. . .] science simply cannot (by its legitimate methods) adjudicate the issue of God's possible superintendence of nature. We neither affirm nor deny it; we simply can't comment on it as scientists. If some of our crowd have made untoward statements claiming that Darwinism disproves God, then I will find Mrs. McInerney and have their knuckles rapped for it (as long as she can equally treat those members of our crowd who have argued that Darwinism must be God's method of action). Science can work only with naturalistic explanations; it can neither affirm nor deny other types of actors (like God) in other spheres.[22]

AJ: It seems a little much that you're willing to say science is a reliable guide when it comes to everything else we know but not when it comes to God. Do you see how suspicious that sounds?

Lucy: It might, if that's what I was saying, but I'm not. There are many things we know to be true that can't be known through science.

AJ: Like what?

Lucy: Okay, do you know that you exist, and that you're having this conversation with me?

AJ: Ah, the joys of philosophical discourse. Yes, of course.

Lucy: Well, that's something you *know* to be true, but not through the scientific method. In fact, science would not be possible if we didn't have other non-scientific forms of knowledge, such as memory, observational knowledge, and linguistic knowledge.[23] Not to mention that science can't prove, or even investigate, the laws of logic, or mathematical truths—it merely presupposes them. And the same is true about morality. Science can't show that we have a duty to help a starving child or that Nazi concentration camps were evil. Good and evil are not material entities that can be measured in a laboratory. But here's the death nail: You're claiming that we shouldn't accept anything as true unless it can be proven true by science, right?

AJ: I think that's what I would have said until this conversation.

Lucy: Ha! It's good to see you're humble. But listen. Even if we weakened the claim to "You shouldn't accept something as true unless it can be supported by scientific evidence," there would still be a problem...

AJ: Because you can't support *that* claim by scientific evidence?[24]

Lucy: Precisely. It's self-defeating. It's careful reasoning we need to use, not science alone. And keep in mind, just yesterday you were using a philosophical argument to show how evil disproves—or makes less likely—the existence of an all-powerful, all-knowing, and all-loving God. If you're open to philosophical arguments disproving the existence of God, shouldn't you be open to philosophical arguments that might prove his existence?

AJ: Okay. Fair enough. But you haven't given me any, so lay them on me, these reasons of yours. I'm an open-minded guy; what I'm after is the truth. What reasons can you give me for God's existence?

Chapter 4

The First Way: Argument from Motion

Lucy: Okay, there are lots of different reasons to believe in God, but I think the most powerful reason is that only God can explain fundamental features of reality. But, I'm not saying God explains things science hasn't figured out.

AJ: Glad to hear it; that would commit the God-of-the-gaps fallacy.

Lucy: Right. And what I'm talking about is different from a God-of-the-gaps. I'm saying that certain features can in principle only be explained by God. Have you ever heard of the Five Ways of St. Thomas Aquinas?

AJ: Funny you should mention them. Yes, I've just been reading about the Five Ways. Surely you can do better than them!

Lucy: Have you? Cool. What's interesting is that the two objections to God's existence you brought up—evil and science being able to account for everything—are actually the two objections Aquinas raises and responds to in the *Summa*.

AJ: The what?

Lucy: The *Summa*. Thomas's greatest work is called the *Summa theologiae*.

It's Latin for "Summary of theology." Anyway, you say I can do better than them? What makes you think they aren't good arguments?

AJ: I thought you said a while back that you'd read *The God Delusion*. Dawkins completely demolishes Aquinas's arguments. I actually have a copy of it here. Listen to this. He writes, "The five 'proofs' asserted by Thomas Aquinas in the thirteenth century don't prove anything, and are easily – though I hesitate to say so, given his eminence – exposed as vacuous."[25] And then he goes through them one by one, knocking them down.

Lucy: Yes, I have read *The God Delusion*. I think Dawkins "misunderstands" rather than "demolishes" Aquinas's arguments. Dawkins commits the straw man fallacy; that is, he refutes a weaker version of his opponent's argument. I don't think he did this intentionally, but as a biologist and not a philosopher, I think he just misunderstood Aquinas. Many atheists do this too. Let's start with the first way Thomas proposes: the argument from motion. What do you take that argument to mean?

AJ: Why don't you refresh my memory.

Lucy: All right. Why don't I look it up and we can read it. Here it is:

> The first and more manifest way is the argument from motion. It is certain, and evident to our senses, that in the world some things are in motion. Now whatever is in motion is put in motion by another, for nothing can be in motion except as it is in potentiality to that towards which it is in motion; whereas a thing moves inasmuch as it is in act. For motion is nothing else than the reduction of something from potentiality to actuality. But nothing can be reduced from potentiality to actuality,

except by something in a state of actuality. Thus that which is actually hot, as fire, makes wood, which is potentially hot, to be actually hot, and thereby moves and changes it.

Now it is not possible that the same thing should be at once in actuality and potentiality in the same respect, but only in different respects. For what is actually hot cannot simultaneously be potentially hot; but it is simultaneously potentially cold. It is therefore impossible that in the same respect and in the same way a thing should be both mover and moved, i.e. that it should move itself. Therefore, whatever is in motion must be put in motion by another. If that by which it is put in motion be itself put in motion, then this also must needs be put in motion by another, and that by another again.

But this cannot go on to infinity, because then there would be no first mover, and, consequently, no other mover; seeing that subsequent movers move only inasmuch as they are put in motion by the first mover; as the staff moves only because it is put in motion by the hand. Therefore it is necessary to arrive at a first mover, put in motion by no other; and this everyone understands to be God.[26]

Okay. So Aquinas is saying that everything we observe is a combination of potentiality and actuality. The water from the faucet is actually liquid, but potentially solid, if we freeze it. A piece of wood before it's put in the fireplace is cool, but it has the potential to get hot and burn if put in the fire. Whenever something goes from potential to actual it must be actualized by something else.

AJ: Sorry to interrupt. When you use the words "potential" and "actual"—I want to make sure I'm understanding you correctly—you mean by "potential" the ability of something to be different than it is, right? And by "actual" you mean how that thing exists at the moment?

Lucy: Yes, "potential" refers to what something can be, while "actuality" refers to what it currently is.

AJ: Okay, but what's his reason for saying "whatever is in motion is put in motion by another"? I don't see how that follows.

Lucy: You agree that the piece of wood, before it goes into the fireplace, is cool and not burning, right?

AJ: Right.

Lucy: And you agree that we would contradict ourselves if we said the wood was both burning and not burning at the same time, right?

AJ: Yeah.

Lucy: Well, then it is impossible for something to be in a state of potentiality and actuality with respect to the same thing at the same time.

AJ: And?

Lucy: And so if the wood isn't hot and burning, it can't cause itself to become hot and burning, because it can't give to itself what it does not have. Therefore, if it undergoes change and becomes hot and burning, it must have been changed by another thing that's actually hot and burning, such as the fire in the fireplace. That's what Thomas means by "whatever is in motion is put in motion by another."

AJ: Okay, let me see if I got this. When something goes from potentiality to actuality, it must be actualized by something else. Water doesn't freeze itself, and wood doesn't light itself on fire. But this chain of movement from the potential to actual can't regress forever. If we keep saying that what actualized the potential in one thing was something else, then we keep shifting the explanation backwards without explaining anything. Is that what you mean?

Lucy: Yes, and that's why Thomas says that "it is necessary to arrive at a first mover, put in motion by no other."

AJ: Can you give me another analogy?

Lucy: All right, consider a train with an infinite number of boxcars; is it moving or standing still? Boxcars can't move themselves, so it must be still. A moving train, however, requires an engine that moves itself and all the other boxcars. Likewise, to explain the change and motion we experience in the universe requires something that is pure actuality. This pure actuality is God.

AJ: Okay, I have two responses. First, even if you're right and an infinite regress is impossible, claiming that whatever stops the regress is "God" is unhelpful at best. You've proven very little about the God you believe exists.

Lucy: We can call the solution to our infinite regress problem "The First Cause" or "Pure Actuality" and then see later whether these terms correspond to the classical understanding of "God." So, you don't have an objection against the argument so much as an application of its conclusion?

AJ: I'm not sure. What do you mean by "*pure* actuality"?

Lucy: It means something that exists in the most perfect way.[27] Things that exist with some potentiality are never fully perfect because there is more that they could become—plus they're dependent on something else to actualize them. But to be pure actuality is to be something that doesn't lack anything, and so it doesn't wait for another to give it something it does not possess already; it is something that doesn't undergo change but rather causes change in other things.

AJ: Yeah, still not sure… But let me make a second point: I have no problem with an infinite regress. What's the issue? Mathematicians in the twenty-first century don't fully comprehend infinity; why assume a medieval monk got it right?

Lucy: It's not enough to say we don't fully comprehend infinity; one could say we are always learning about many concepts. What mistake does Thomas make in his argument? Isn't it possible that what we've learned about infinity since Thomas's time has confirmed rather than refuted his position?

AJ: Look, I'm not a mathematician any more than you are. I just don't see the problem in having causes that stretch back forever. You ask, what mistake does Thomas make? He too quickly rules out the possibility of an infinite regress of movers. If you want to hang your hat on Thomas's medieval views on reality, fine; but I'm not convinced.

Lucy: Let's try a simple thought experiment. Imagine a chandelier that's one link short of reaching the ceiling. If you let it go, it falls, right?

AJ: Yes, it would fall to the ground.

Lucy: Okay. Suppose the ceiling is thousands of feet high. So you add ten thousand more links to the chain. But it's still one chain link short, so—and this is important—the chain is only being held up by other links. With ten thousand links, it still falls.

AJ: I'm following.

Lucy: Let's think of a higher ceiling. How about a million more links or a billion; if it doesn't reach the ceiling, it still falls. Now, suppose there is an infinite number of links in the chain; after every link, there is another, but the ceiling is always one link away.

AJ: You'd have an infinitely high A/C bill for this ridiculously big home. Is that your point?

Lucy: Let's be serious.

AJ: Sorry, continue.

Lucy: Even with an infinite number of links, those are the only things holding up the chandelier. If we agree that billions or trillions of links in this chain can't by themselves hold up the chandelier, then how could an infinite number of them do that? We've already seen that adding more links in the chain doesn't help solve the problem. To keep the chandelier up, we need something that doesn't depend on anything else to stay up. Chains, by their nature, can't do that, but a ceiling can.

AJ: Okay.

Lucy: The same is true in the universe. An infinite number of movers doesn't explain the motion we observe; only an unmoved mover, something that causes motion in others but receives it from none, can explain that. Similarly, it makes no sense to hold that things in motion move themselves. No being can be in a state of actuality and potentiality with respect to the same thing at the same time. Therefore, if it's in a state of potentiality, it can't actualize itself, but it must be actualized by another. So at the end of the day, you have to accept an unmoved mover. I'm happy to hear your thoughts on that, and then maybe we can talk about Thomas's other ways for proving God's existence.

AJ: Okay, I don't mean to sound flippant, but I'm not buying it. First, using a mundane example like a chandelier is misleading. I'm not saying you're intending to be misleading, but I think it is misleading. Yeah, we understand how everyday things like chain links and chandeliers and even gravity work, but to say that we therefore can conclude that the universe must be like a ceiling seems a little trite. We know so very little about this universe; I'm not going to be convinced by these sorts of examples. Maybe there could be an infinite number of movers, and if there is, whether or not that makes sense to you, you'll have to learn to deal with it because that's reality.

You said Thomas had five proofs? Why don't you move on to the second one now?

Lucy: Before we do, you said you were open-minded and willing to be proven wrong. Yet, when confronted with evidence for God, you say there's a lot we don't understand. So here's a question: Is there anything at all, in theory, that would show you God exists and that you couldn't respond to with, "Well, we don't understand how everything works, so maybe it's not God"? It just seems to me like your atheism has something in common with some religious beliefs: it can't be falsified.

AJ: Oh, that's easy. God could appear in the sky right now, and with a big booming voice say, "AJ, I exist! You were wrong to be an atheist. Lucy is right; listen to her, you idiot!"

Lucy: Really? A booming voice? How do you know it's God and not aliens, the government, or an eccentric billionaire? Saying "It's God" doesn't really tell us anything.

AJ: I think I'd just believe it is God because . . . Well, I was going to say that would be more plausible than aliens, but I don't think that. Let's say there were no signs of aliens and I had no signs of being mentally deranged. I think I'd just accept that it is true, whether or not you think I should; I think I just would. . . .

Lucy: Don't you think an argument for God based on what we observe in the world is stronger than hearing a strange voice one time?

AJ: Well, then explain why God didn't provide evidence that he exists in the natural world that everyone could access. In fact—that's another great reason to think he doesn't exist! Because if he did, surely he'd know what would convince people and he'd do it.

Lucy: The evidence *is* there, AJ. But that doesn't mean it's going to be easy to argue for God's existence. The Church teaches that God's existence *can* be known by human reason, but that does not mean everyone will come to that knowledge.[28] Aquinas certainly thought many people would not, and that's why God revealed himself as well.[29]

AJ: Maybe we should move on to the second proof?

Lucy: I hate to be the one to flee the battlefield, but I actually have to go.

AJ: Haha, no problem, Lucy. I'll be sure to look over ol' Tommy boy's second way tonight. Do you want to meet at the same time tomorrow?

Lucy: Sounds good to me. But if I'm educating you, the least you can do is buy my coffee, okay?

AJ: Let's call it entertainment, and sure.

Chapter 5

The Second Way: Argument from Efficient Causality

Lucy: Wow! You're looking chipper this morning.

AJ: Neeed Coffeeeeeee!

Lucy: Haha. I'll be waiting for you.

***

AJ: Business idea, Lucy.

Lucy: What's that?

AJ: A coffee shop where you get to hook up to an IV of coffee until reality becomes bearable.

Lucy: Big night, huh?

AJ: Something like that.

Lucy: Well, you let me know when you've come back to your happy place. I'm just studying for a test.

AJ: I'm ready, I'm ready. I told you I'd look up Aquinas's second way last night, which I did.

Lucy: And?

AJ: And it's exactly the same as his first argument.

Lucy: Now if that were true, why would Thomas have bothered putting it forward?

AJ: I don't know; maybe "the 5 ways" sounded cooler than "the 4"?

Lucy: Yeah, no. You're right that the two arguments are similar, but that shouldn't surprise us since in both arguments—as well as in the other three—Thomas is arguing from what we observe in the world to the conclusion that God exists. The first way had to do with motion; this one has to do with efficient causality.

AJ: You have it there?

Lucy: I do. Let me read it:

> The second way is from the nature of the efficient cause. In the world of sense we find there is an order of efficient causes. There is no case known (neither is it, indeed, possible) in which a thing is found to be the efficient cause of itself; for so it would be prior to itself, which is impossible. Now in efficient causes it is not possible to go on to infinity, because in all efficient causes following in order, the first is the cause of the intermediate cause, and the intermediate is the cause of the ultimate cause, whether the intermediate cause be several, or only one. Now to take away the cause is to take away the effect. Therefore, if there be no first cause among efficient causes, there will be no ultimate, nor any intermediate cause. But if in efficient causes it is possible to go on to infinity, there will be no first efficient cause, neither will there be an ultimate effect, nor any intermediate efficient causes;

all of which is plainly false. Therefore it is necessary to admit a first efficient cause, to which everyone gives the name of God.[30]

AJ: Here's the thing, Lucy—and I'd be surprised if you didn't see this coming—if everything needs a cause, who caused God? Why is God the exception?

Lucy: Where does St. Thomas say that everything needs a cause?

AJ: That's kinda the point of the argument, no?

Lucy: No. Thomas isn't saying whatever *is* needs a cause; he's saying whatever is caused is caused by *another*. His point is that an infinite regress of causes dependent on other causes will not explain the effect we observe; so there must be a first cause that is uncaused, which we call God.

AJ: He's still going on about this infinite regress stuff. Honestly, the argument sounds like a less convincing and way more confusing version of William Lane Craig's Kalām cosmological argument, except whereas Craig talks about time, Thomas talks about causes.[31]

Lucy: Well, the difference between Craig and Thomas is that Craig believes that one can give philosophical arguments for the beginning of the universe; Thomas doesn't.

AJ: Really?

Lucy: Really. Aquinas believes the world began to exist because of Divine Revelation—the Bible teaches it—but he does not think you can prove the universe had a beginning philosophically.[32] And, of course, big bang cosmology wasn't a thing in Thomas's day. All of the five ways, including this one, do not assume the universe had a beginning.

AJ: Okay, now I'm confused. He's saying…wait…what's he saying?

Lucy: An efficient cause is one that either causes the existence of a thing or causes a change in a thing. Two examples: Your parents were the efficient cause of you. Without them you wouldn't have existence. A fire that warms a person in the winter is the efficient cause of the warmth of the person, even though the person remains a person the entire time.

AJ: Okay. I still don't see how this is different from Craig's argument. Thomas is saying that things that were caused were caused by things before them, and that those things, the causers, also had causers, but that this can't stretch back infinitely because if it did there wouldn't be a first efficient cause. Correct?

Lucy: No. That *isn't* what St. Thomas is arguing. Remember, Thomas isn't trying to prove the world had a beginning. Perhaps you're right; perhaps the past is infinite. If it is, then there exists before you, let's say, an infinite number of efficient causes that eventually resulted in you, AJ, being conceived by your parents. But that isn't what Thomas is concerned with, because that's a linear or accidentally ordered series of causes, which are spread out over a historical timeline. What Thomas is referring to is a hierarchically or essentially ordered series of causes, which do not regress into the past.

AJ: Man, I need another coffee. What's the difference?

Lucy: Think of it this way: A hierarchically or essentially ordered series of causes is one like the links in the chandelier chain. Each link in the chain is dependent not only on the one link above it, but on every link above it. At a given moment in time, all the links are present and, together with the ceiling, are holding up the chandelier. If it weren't for the ceiling, none of those links could hold up the chandelier. However, a linear or accidentally ordered series of causes is different. In a linear series of causes, a member of the series is not continually dependent on *all* of the previous causes in the chain. Instead, a member of a linear series is dependent on the cause directly previous to it—but *only during the time it is being caused.* After that it can act causally on its own, independently of *all* the causes previous to it. For example, even if your father did not exist now, AJ, you could still have a child, and, God forbid you died early after your son was born, your son could still grow up and one day have a child. Aquinas thinks that God could create a world where an infinite number of accidentally ordered causes exist, even though you think he is denying that. But what Thomas is really denying is an infinite regress of hierarchically or essentially ordered efficient causes—because then the observed effect could not exist.[33] Does that make sense?

AJ: Let me see if I'm understanding this. Man, this is a lot first thing in the morning. I love it. Okay, after my son is born, he's no longer dependent on me to act as a cause. Even at a later time after I've died, my son can, along with a woman, produce—cause—a son of his own. However, this isn't true in an essentially ordered series of causes, such as several gears all moving, let's say, because the handle is being turned. In that case, if you stop moving the handle, all of the gears cease moving simultaneously because each gear in the series is receiving its causal power from each and *every* other gear prior to it, all the way up to the first cause. And your big point, I guess, is that the first cause must have causal power in itself—it does not receive it from another—otherwise, none of the gears would have any causal power.

Lucy: Couldn't have said it better myself, yes. Thomas is using cause in that second sense, the gears-turning sense. The same is true for his first way. That's why I used the example yesterday of an infinite series of boxcars, remember? But wait a minute…I just thought of something better. Pass me that book there.

AJ: It's *The God Delusion*, hope that's okay.

Lucy: Using *The God Delusion* to help make the case for God will be a joy. Okay, now, notice that my hand is pushing the book, and the book is pushing the cup. My hand is a first cause relative to this series of causation. Without my hand, the book would have no causal power to move the cup, right?

AJ: Right.

Lucy: Now, we know my hand isn't a first cause in an absolute sense because it's caused as well by the motion of my arm. So my hand is one more intermediate—or instrumental—cause in this essentially ordered causal series. So now we have the motion of my arm serving as a first cause relative to the series involving my hand, the book, and the cup. Without the motion of my arm, both my hand and the book cease in their causal activity because both my hand and the book are entirely dependent on the causal power of my arm in order to exercise their causal activity.

AJ: So your arm is the first cause?

Lucy: Not in an absolute sense, because it's caused as well by the flexing of the muscles, which in turn is caused by the firing of neurons in the brain, etc. Okay, now consider a scenario where there is no first cause relative to the entire or whole essentially ordered series of causes—a series where every cause is an intermediate cause, which is what an infinite regression suggests—no absolute first cause. Would any instrumental or intermediate cause in the causal series have any causal power?

AJ: You want me to say no.

Lucy: It couldn't have any causal power. If the Person doesn't move the arm, then the arm has no causal power, and if the arm doesn't move the book, then the book has no causal power, which means the cup wouldn't move—but we observe the cup moving. So there must be a first cause of this essentially ordered causal series that is uncaused.[34]

AJ: Are you saying that God helps you to move the cup?!

Lucy: Well, in a sense, yes.

AJ: That's ridiculous! How are you not just a puppet, then?

Lucy: I admit it's complicated, but we do have freedom of choice.

AJ: I don't see how, if God's doing everything.

Lucy: I'm not saying God is *doing* everything; otherwise, humans would be puppets. What I'm saying is that God *actualizes* humans in such a way as to make free choice possible. Here's an analogy. You can drive a car anywhere you choose, but you can't drive at all without gasoline. Similarly, God supplies you with the "energy"—the actuality—that you need to make a choice, but He leaves it up to you to choose what you want.[35]

AJ: I need another coffee. Do me a favor: sum it up for me here, Lucy. Your complicated—which doesn't mean sophisticated, by the way—theology is confusing.

Lucy: Okay, so to sum up, I'd say (1) If infinite regression (no first cause of an essentially ordered series of causes), then intermediate/instrumental causes would have no causal power. But (2) intermediate/instrumental causes do have causal power, because we see they are producing an effect. (3) Therefore, there must exist a first cause that is uncaused.

AJ: Yeah... all of that still sounds like the first way to me, like when Aquinas says the staff only moves because of the hand.

Lucy: That's because the second way is more general—it covers *any* kind of order of efficient causes, even the one in the first way. But Thomas does take the second way in a new direction when he says that it is impossible for a thing to be the efficient cause of itself. Instead of focusing on accidental changes in a substance, as in the first way, the second way can be used to argue for a first cause of substances themselves.

AJ: Can you give me an example?

Lucy: Sure. Take this gold cross necklace my mother gave me. This piece of gold is a substance made up of gold atoms. The gold atoms are efficiently caused by particles—electrons, neutrons, and protons. The protons are efficiently caused by quarks—three to each proton, and the quarks...

AJ: Are efficiently caused by superstrings?

Lucy: That's one theory. But Aquinas's point is that these efficient causes cannot regress infinitely; otherwise, the piece of gold you see in front of you would not exist. So there must be a first uncaused cause that explains the existence of the substance gold.

AJ: I think my brain has had all that it can handle for one morning. And...I'm running out of coffee. But I do want to think more about that last point you made.

Lucy: Okay, well, why don't we break for today then. You can think it over and we'll meet back up tomorrow. Sound good?

AJ: Yeah, that sounds good.

Chapter 6

The Third Way: Argument from Possibility and Necessity

AJ: Hey, Lucy. Coffee?

Lucy: Good to see you. I'm okay, just got one.

AJ: Okay, give me one sec.

***

AJ: How are you?

Lucy: I'm good, I'm good, thanks. I brought a copy of the *Summa* this time.

AJ: That's big!

Lucy: That's the first part of a five-volume set.

AJ: Well, there you go! Want to read the third way?

Lucy: Sure.

> The third way is taken from possibility and necessity, and runs
> thus. We find in nature things that are possible to be and not
> to be, since they are found to be generated, and to corrupt,
> and consequently, they are possible to be and not to be. But it
> is impossible for these always to exist, for that which is pos-

sible not to be at some time is not. Therefore, if everything is possible not to be, then at one time there could have been nothing in existence.

Now if this were true, even now there would be nothing in existence, because that which does not exist only begins to exist by something already existing.

Therefore, if at one time nothing was in existence, it would have been impossible for anything to have begun to exist; and thus even now nothing would be in existence—which is absurd. Therefore, not all beings are merely possible, but there must exist something the existence of which is necessary. But every necessary thing either has its necessity caused by another, or not. Now it is impossible to go on to infinity in necessary things which have their necessity caused by another, as has been already proved in regard to efficient causes.

Therefore we cannot but postulate the existence of some being having of itself its own necessity, and not receiving it from another, but rather causing in others their necessity. This all men speak of as God.[36]

All right, let's examine what Aquinas is saying in everything we just read. First, can we agree there are things that don't have to exist, like rocks or planets, or people—contingent things? And can we agree, in theory, that there could be things which have to exist or can't not exist—necessary things? "Have to exist" and "don't have to exist" seem pretty exhaustive, don't you think?

AJ: Whoa! Too much, too fast. I think I know what you mean by a contingent being, but I'm not totally sure. What do you mean some beings have existence contingently?

Lucy: Sure. Let me give you an example. Without your parents, AJ, you wouldn't exist. So, your existence is contingent because you were dependent on a cause for your existence—actually two causes, Mom and Dad. Therefore, you are a possible being.

AJ: Actually, I was grown artificially in a lab as part of a secret government project...

Lucy: Uh huh.

AJ: Not a sci-fi fan, huh? Look, I know I was dependent on my parents to exist, and that I didn't exist before I was conceived. . . .

Lucy: What is it? . . .

AJ: I just heard what I said and thought how funny it would be if someone was overhearing us.

Lucy: Ha! Like you said, the joy of philosophical discourse.

AJ: Sorry, as I was saying, I get that I didn't exist before I was conceived, but I'm made of matter, and maybe that matter has always existed and so we don't need to posit God.

Lucy: Well, Thomas's point is that because things are generated, such as you from your parents, we know something, indirectly, about their existence—that it is contingent. Because if your existence were not contingent, then it would be necessary, which means you would have always existed. But clearly that isn't true about you, so you're a possible being.

AJ: Yeah, but what about the view that I'm made of matter and matter has always existed. So, matter is the necessary being and we don't need God…Well?

Lucy: I heard you. I'm trying to take in what you said. Do you really think the only difference between you and a stone is just a different arrangement of electrons and protons? That your life, your consciousness, your intelligence—and even your humor—are nothing more than electrons spinning and chemicals interacting?

AJ: Well, when you put it that way, it doesn't sound so flattering—but it could be true nonetheless! Besides, I've never seen a good argument for the soul; I think consciousness comes from the brain. But you're not addressing my point, Lucy. If matter always existed, then matter is the necessary being and we don't need God.

Lucy: You remember that Thomas said human reason can't prove the universe did not always exist, right?

AJ: Yeah.

Lucy: So, let's say you're correct and matter has always existed—that still wouldn't make it the kind of Necessary Being that Aquinas argues God is.

AJ: So, there are different kinds of necessary beings? And matter is only one of them?

Lucy: Let me try an analogy. Imagine that the sun, which gives light to our galaxy, always existed. It always was, it is now, and it always will be. It would be a necessary being, right?

AJ: Right.

Lucy: Now, the light coming out of the sun would also always exist, so it also would be a necessary being—but there is a difference. . .

AJ: Ahh. . . I get it. So, the light would still be dependent on the sun for its existence. The light is a necessary being, but only through the sun.

Lucy: Exactly. Thomas says some necessary beings are necessary through another, but they all can't be like that. There has to be something that is necessary through itself, not through another.

AJ: And you're saying matter is necessary through another. But why? Why can't matter just always exist through itself?

Lucy: If I promise to address that later, can we get back to the reasoning of the third way?

AJ: Alright, but I'm gonna hold you to it.

Lucy: Fine. But for now, do you agree that you, AJ, are a possible being?

AJ: Yeah, but my matter might be a necessary being.

Lucy: Forget about *your* matter. I'm talking about *you*. You are a unique person that has not always existed, and who was dependent on your parents for your existence. If your parents never met, you wouldn't exist. You're an example of a possible being—at the very least, you understand, now, what I mean by a "possible being," right?

AJ: Sure.

Lucy: Okay, so, consider this thought experiment. Is it possible that everything which exists is a possible being?

AJ: I guess you would say no.

Lucy: That's right, and do you know why?

AJ: Because a possible being only comes to exist through an already existing cause external to it; but if everything were a possible being, then there'd be no way to explain how they came into existence in the first place.

Lucy: That's it! As Thomas says, "it would have been impossible for anything to have begun to exist" in our imagined scenario of a universe of only possible beings. And if nothing could have begun to exist, then there would've been nothing in the past. But if there were nothing in the past, then nothing would exist now. But this is absurd, as Thomas says, because things do exist now. You and I are talking; we're sitting in a coffee shop. Therefore, at least one necessary being must exist.

AJ: Listen, thought experiments are fun and all, but they don't always tell us something about the real world. I prefer an empirical approach.

Lucy: I understand that, but notice that Thomas is coming to his conception of a possible being from the knowledge we have of things in the *real* world. When a new baby is born, we know that it's a contingent, or possible, being. Since possible beings exist in the world, it's legitimate to ask the question, can all the things that exist be possible beings?

AJ: Okay, but I can think of a few problems here.

Lucy: Such as…

AJ: Maybe the first possible being caused itself, and that started the whole causal chain.

Lucy: Thomas ruled that out in the second way, remember? Something can't be the efficient cause of itself. You're giving me that look…

AJ: I hear what you're saying, but it's not clicking. Maybe I'm just not used to the terminology. It's like learning a new language.

Lucy: It is. But let me put it this way. No thing can be the cause of its own existence because it would already have to exist in order to act as a cause of its own existence. But if it already exists, then it does not need to cause its own existence.

AJ: That makes more sense to me. I mean, I agree that *I* could not have caused myself to exist. But maybe things can arise from nothing. You've heard, I'm sure, that Lawrence Krauss talks about this in his book *A Universe from Nothing*—that things can come into existence out of nothing.[37] So even if it's true that there was once a state of nothingness, if my only options are (1) God made the universe or (2) it came out of nothing—and since we've got good reasons from modern physics to think this can happen—I'd choose option two.

Lucy: Krauss does a bait-and-switch with nothing. By "nothing" I mean the complete absence of anything, while Krauss means a vacuum that has only unstable quantum energy—not matter—in it.[38] That's not nothing.[39] Thomas's point is that if there were truly nothing in the past, there would be nothing now, but things do exist now. So, at least one necessary being must exist. If you just say, "Something can come from nothing because I can imagine it," then we're back to unfalsifiable atheism—booming voices or angels proclaiming God could just come from nothing too—plus that view would destroy science.

AJ: How would it destroy science?

Lucy: Well, think about it. Science is about cause and effect relationships, right?

AJ: Right.

Lucy: But if things can come into existence without a cause—that is, from nothing, the complete absence of anything—then science is undermined. There'd be no more need for causal explanations. We could just say, "It just magically appeared from nothing." Even though nothing has *no properties*, somehow it can cause anything and everything. Why do we need science if that's true? This is the "God-of-the-gaps" in reverse. The "Gap"—nothing— explains why everything exists.

AJ: What if nothing, in the way you're using the word, can't exist? What if the only "nothing" there is, is what Krauss refers to? Why think your "nothing" has to exist?

Lucy: What if we live in a computer simulation? What if we never landed on the moon? We can do "what if" all day. But Thomas begins the third way, not with "what if" but with "it's a fact that" there are possible beings. From this, it's natural to raise the question, why do they exist? Indeed, the question, why is there something rather than nothing whatsoever? has been debated by philosophers for many centuries; it's not some silly question to be quickly dismissed.[40]

AJ: We can ask "what if" all day, but honestly—and I think this is one of the major differences between you and me—I'm okay not knowing. I'm okay with mystery. You—and try not to take this too offensively—need a Bible and a God to make your world neat, ordered, and, well, unmysterious. But for the sake of argument, however, I'll grant your point. Let's say Krauss is doing a bait-and-switch, like you say, and things can't come into existence out of nothing. You still haven't told me how many necessary beings there are, which one I should call God, and why matter can't be the necessary being in place of God.

Lucy: I'm not offended, but I find it strange that someone like yourself who loves science seems so ready to give up the search for causes and embrace mystery. But let me get back on topic. I want to address those points of yours, as I promised. The second part of the third way says, "But every necessary thing either has its necessity caused by another, or not. Now it is impossible to go on to infinity in necessary things which have their necessity caused by another, as has been already proved in regard to efficient causes…"[41]

AJ: Wait… He's referring to the second way when he says "as has been already proved in regard to efficient causes," right?

Lucy: Yes. Remember, last time we realized that if there is no first cause in an essentially ordered series of causes, then the intermediate/instrumental causes would have no causal power. Likewise, if there's no being that's necessary through itself, then there'd be no beings that are necessary from another. So, Thomas's point in the third way is that we cannot have an infinite regress of beings that are necessary through another; instead, there must be "some being having of itself its own necessity, and not receiving it from another, but rather causing in others their necessity. This all men speak of as God."[42]

AJ: Okay, I get it that there has to be at least one being that is necessary through itself. But maybe there are several beings that are necessary, each through itself. And why should we call any of them God? And, not to beat a dead horse, but you still haven't told me why matter can't be the being that is necessary through itself.

Lucy: Well, to the extent that the being that is necessary through itself is responsible for the existence of all other things, this sounds a lot like God the Creator. As for matter…

AJ: Hold on. That would follow if there's *only one being* that's necessary through itself—but what if there are multiple beings that are necessary, each through itself?

Lucy: That's a good point, AJ. But Thomas argues there cannot be more than one being that is necessary through itself. Let me read you the passage from his other *Summa*.

AJ: How many *Summas* did this guy write!?

Lucy: This *guy* also wrote the *Summa contra gentiles*, and here's what he wrote that responds to your question: "If there are two beings of which both are necessary beings, they must agree in the notion of the necessity of being. Hence, they must be distinguished by something added either to one of them only, or to both. This means that one or both of them must be composite. Now, as we have shown, no composite being is through itself a necessary being. It is impossible therefore that there be many beings of which each is a necessary being. Hence, neither can there be many gods."[43]

AJ: And that means what, exactly?

Lucy: Every composite being is dependent on its parts for its existence. For example, a painting is composed of a canvas and paint. This means that every composite is caused by something else, because something must cause these different parts to unite.[44] So, we can't have more than one being that is necessary through itself, because in order for there to be two such beings, one must have a property that the other does not have—otherwise they would *not* be two different beings, but one and the same being. But if one has a property the other does not have, then it is actually a composite being. But every composite being needs a cause, so a composite being can't be a being that is necessary through itself.

AJ: And matter is a composite being, so it can't be a being that's necessary through itself—is that your point?

Lucy: That's my point.

AJ: How do you know that?

Lucy: Because matter undergoes change, which means it's a composite of actuality and potentiality—and that means it's caused by another. As we've seen in the first way, a thing cannot actualize its own potentiality because the same thing can't be both in potentiality with respect to something and in actuality with respect to the same thing at the same time. This means that when matter is actualized there must be a cause external to it, or, as Thomas puts it, what is changed is changed by another. But a being that has existence necessarily through itself does not and *cannot* rely on any other cause for anything.

AJ: So, at best, the material universe could have always existed, but it would still be dependent on a being that's necessary through itself, which you call God.

Lucy: Yes.

AJ: And I suppose you'd say the same thing about a singularity in Big Bang theory—that at best it could only be a being that's necessary through another, not necessary through itself.

Lucy: Yes, and like matter, it would also be a composite being—a mixture of actuality and potentiality—because it would have within it the potential to expand into the physical universe we see today.

AJ: Hmm… that's a whole lot to think about! But we'll have to continue this discussion tomorrow, Lucy. My friends and I are going out tonight, and I have to run home to get ready.

Lucy: Sounds good, AJ. Enjoy the weekend! Same time, Monday?

AJ: I'll be here.

Chapter 7
The Value of Objections

Lucy: Hi, AJ. Did you enjoy the weekend?

AJ: Oh, yes!

Lucy: Look at you in such a good mood, and before coffee! I suppose you're eager to get into the fourth way, huh?

AJ: Maybe later. Before we get to that, I want to bring something up. I spent the weekend with some of my friends, and we talked a lot about the five ways—actually, the first three ways that you and I discussed. And I think there are some real problems you are missing.

Lucy: Really... Do these friends of yours study philosophy?

AJ: One of them does. He's an atheist like me.

Lucy: Alright, let's hear about these problems I'm missing.

AJ: Give me a sec.

Lucy: Ah, you wrote notes. This is going to be good.

AJ: Where should I begin? I don't know why I didn't think of this earlier, but the first three ways are useless towards proving the God of Christianity.

Lucy: I never said that they prove Christianity. They only prove a thin slice of God, you could say; they also support some other monotheistic religions.

AJ: Right, I thought you'd say that. That's not what I'm talking about. The problem with the three arguments we've looked at is that they could just as easily prove the existence of three Gods, which would disprove monotheism. Even if I grant that the first way proves an unmoved mover, the second way an uncaused cause, and the third way a necessary being—how do I know that these are not proving the existence of three different gods?

Lucy: Well, three gods are better than none…

AJ: Not for a monotheist, like you. But wait, I'm not finished. It's also not even clear that the first way is successful in arguing for just one cause that is pure actuality. Aquinas took the first way from Aristotle, correct?

Lucy: Correct.[45]

AJ: Well, let me read to you what Aristotle says. Like Thomas, he argues there must be—and I'm quoting him here—"a principle, whose very essence is actuality."[46] He describes it as a "substance which is eternal and unmovable and separate from sensible things."[47]

Lucy: Okay. I'm impressed that you're reading Aristotle, but I have to confess that I don't see where this is going…

AJ: You will. I haven't finished yet. Aristotle continues, "But we must not ignore the question whether we have to suppose one such substance or more than one, and if the latter, how many…"[48] And then he argues that they number fifty-five or forty-seven, adding, "Let this, then, be taken as the number of the spheres, so that the unmovable substances and principles also may probably be taken as just so many."[49]

Lucy: So what? Aristotle has an outdated view of the universe.

AJ: Well, now, so does Aquinas. Didn't he believe that the Earth was at the center of the universe?

Lucy: Yes.[50]

AJ: But just because Aquinas was wrong about that, it doesn't follow that his metaphysics was off, does it?

Lucy: Fair enough.

AJ: Aquinas is giving a similar argument about pure actuality. But Aristotle thinks there can be 47 or 55 pure actualities. What is Aquinas's argument for why there can be only one pure actuality?

Lucy: Well, Thomas must understand the first way differently than Aristotle.

AJ: Fine, then explain the difference to me.

Lucy: Well... Look, to be honest...

AJ: ...You don't know?

Lucy: I don't.

AJ: Well, then how does Aquinas argue that the pure actuality of the first way, the uncaused cause of the second way, and the necessary being of the third way are one and the same being? Do you know his argument for that?

Lucy: Not offhand, no.

AJ: It seems you know a lot less than you thought you knew, Lucy. Maybe you need to take back the claim that the five ways prove monotheism....

You're not saying anything....

Lucy: That's because you've stumped me. Happy?

AJ: Thrilled! And to be honest, I think it's cool that you can admit it.

Lucy: Thanks, I guess… You've reminded me how humbling philosophy can be. There is so much to know and so much I don't know…. But I'm sorta glad this happened, you know? It proves why it's so important to talk with people of differing opinions—it's how we grow. Unfortunately, nowadays many people just yell at each other without really listening.

AJ: Haha, well, I've been humbled too. Remember that shirt I was wearing the day we first met? "I'm an Atheist, debate me!" Totally was not expecting to meet a Christian who could actually take me up on that challenge.

Lucy: Ha! Well, thanks.

AJ: You forced me to really think about these things, and that's helped me a lot. Do you have any idea how long I was up on atheist online forums last night? How about you consider the questions I raised, and we can talk more about them tomorrow?

Lucy: Sounds good. Thanks, AJ.

AJ: No prob. See you tomorrow.

***

AJ: You're here bright and early!

Lucy: I am.

AJ: You look tired.

Lucy: Thanks a lot! Because of you, I've been up most of the night reading more about Thomas Aquinas—and I even called one of my old philosophy professors.

AJ: You have his personal number?

Lucy: His office number.

AJ: Right… So, I'm guessing you think you can respond to my objections?

Lucy: I think so.

AJ: Alright, well, let me grab a coffee and you'll have my undivided attention.

***

AJ: Alright, why am I wrong?

Lucy: Your arguments reflect a common misunderstanding of Thomas Aquinas—that he's nothing more than a glorified Aristotelian.

AJ: I thought that's how you Catholics thought of him. Aristotle on steroids.

Lucy: He uses similar language, but there are important differences. For example, Thomas understands the word "being" very differently.[51]

AJ: How so?

Lucy: Well, simply put, for Thomas, being is primarily about existence, whereas for Aristotle being is primarily about essence.

AJ: Explain.

Lucy: Okay. You know what a dinosaur is?

AJ: Did you really just ask me that question?

Lucy: Fair enough, but indulge me.

AJ: Yes, I know what dinosaurs are. Large reptiles that lived hundreds of millions of years ago.

Lucy: Right. Now let me ask you a second question. Do dinosaurs exist now?

AJ: No, Lucy, dinosaurs do not exist now.

Lucy: You've just illustrated the distinction between essence and existence. Essence concerns what kind of thing something is—a plant, a reptile, a human being. But the question, does X exist? can't be answered in the same way. That question must be answered with a "yes," "no," or "maybe." Aquinas's philosophy stresses the importance of existence over essence, so his five ways must be interpreted in an *existential* way, not in an *essential* way, as for Aristotle.[52]

AJ: I don't understand how this overcomes the problems I mentioned yesterday.

Lucy: Well, you asked how Aristotle could claim there are as many as 47 or 55 pure actualities, and yet Thomas is a monotheist, right?

AJ: Right.

Lucy: Well, Aristotle understands nature or essence primarily as form.[53] Humans and dogs are both made of matter, but they are different kinds of beings due to having different forms. The form is what actualizes the matter, making it the kind of thing it is. Since Aristotle understood actuality as form, there can be multiple pure forms or essences, which would differ in kind just as plants, reptiles, and humans differ in kind. But if actuality is understood as existence, there can be only one pure existence.

AJ: Okay, you're gonna have to slow down. Why should I believe that existence is more important than essence? I don't even know what it means to say that God is pure existence or how one would argue for that—but you're gonna have to argue for that. Plus, you need to explain how there can only be one thing that is pure existence—and then you still won't be done. You also have to show that the first way, the second way, and the third way are all talking about this one pure existence. Are you going to be able to do all of that?

Lucy: Yes. You better grab another coffee, AJ, because this is going to take a while.

AJ: Give me a sec…. It's time for a double espresso. You want something?

Lucy: I'll have the same, thanks.

***

AJ: Okay. Here you go. I'm ready.

Lucy: I think it'll be easiest if I start with the third way.

AJ: Okay.

Lucy: Okay, in the third way Thomas focuses on the fact that some things are generated, such as human beings by parents, which shows that they have existence contingently. For if they had existence necessarily, then they would have always existed. But the fact that they didn't always exist means that their existence isn't something they get from possessing human nature or essence.

AJ: Sorry to interrupt. But their essence is what again?

Lucy: Essence refers to the kind of being something is. Humans are rational animals, or rational mammals, if you prefer.

AJ: And humans don't get existence from their essence—but what do they get from their essence?

Lucy: Essence concerns the properties you have necessarily. One example of a property we get from our essence is life, because to be human is to be a living thing. So, it is in our nature, or essence, to be alive.

AJ: Ah, okay... But how can an essence, which is a concept, give us properties?

Lucy: Alright, I guess my sleep deprivation is preventing me from explaining this as well as I could. Let me try again: In our minds, we think about the essence human through a concept, which we abstract from our experience of human beings. But this concept isn't just made up; instead, it reflects, in a general way, the essence human as it *exists* in the individual humans we see every day.[54]

AJ: Okay. So, you're saying that the essence human can exist in an individual person, like me, and it can also exist in my mind, as a concept.

Lucy: Yes, the essence *human* exists in you, AJ, because you *are* a human being, not a dog. But the essence human exists in you in a concrete way, for you are an actually existing, individual human being. However, when you try to understand the essence human in your mind, you focus on *rational animal* in an abstract or general way.

AJ: Alright. So, the essence can be thought about in our minds, but what we think about reflects reality. I exist as a human being, not a dog. Rational animal expresses my essence, or the kind of being that I am.

Lucy: That's right. Now, if existence were included in your essence or nature, that would mean that you would always exist—just as it's in the essence of a triangle to always have three sides. But that can't be true, because we know that human beings are generated by parents and eventually die, which shows that they have existence contingently. This means that humans are possible beings; it is possible for them to exist and not to exist. And that means that humans don't get existence from their essence, but instead their existence must be caused in them by an external cause. Remember, as

Thomas argued, a possible being cannot cause its own existence, because then it would exist prior to itself, which is impossible. But if everything were a possible being, then there'd be no way to explain how possible beings came into existence in the first place. Therefore, at least one necessary being must exist.

AJ: We went over this before; I don't see how this is new…

Lucy: What's new is the existential interpretation of the first three ways that I didn't appreciate last time, which I'm getting to now…

AJ: Okay, continue.

Lucy: In order for a possible being to acquire existence, there must be a cause that possesses existence necessarily, not contingently. And a hierarchical regress of beings that get their necessity from another would not explain how any of them have existence necessarily. Thus, there must be a first cause that has its necessary existence only from itself. And the only way this is possible is if its essence and existence are identical. In other words, God isn't some kind of essence, such as human, which *has* existence. Instead, God *is* existence itself. Let me read to you how Thomas argues for this:

> Whatever a thing has besides its essence must be caused either by the constituent principles of that essence (like a property that necessarily accompanies the species—as the faculty of laughing is proper to a man—and is caused by the constituent principles of the species), or by some exterior agent—as heat is caused in water by fire. Therefore, if the existence of a thing differs from its essence, this existence must be caused either by some exterior agent or by its essential principles. Now it is im-

possible for a thing's existence to be caused by its essential constituent principles, for nothing can be the sufficient cause of its own existence, if its existence is caused. Therefore that thing, whose existence differs from its essence, must have its existence caused by another. But this can't be true of God; because we call God the first efficient cause. Therefore it is impossible that in God His existence should differ from His essence.[55]

AJ: How does this help defend monotheism, again?

Lucy: There can only be one being that is existence itself, and so only one God.

AJ: You know you're going to have to argue for that, Lucy.

Lucy: I know. I can now give an existential version of the argument from the *Summa contra gentiles*, which I gave last time. Here it is. In order for there to be two beings that are pure existence, one must have a property that the other does not have—otherwise they would *not* be two different beings, but one and the same being. But if one has a property the other does not have, then it is actually a composite of existence and *some property*—and not *pure* existence after all. Every composite being needs a cause, so a composite being cannot be a being that is necessary through itself.

AJ: I don't see why there can't be two pure existences, just as, for example, identical twin babies exist.

Lucy: Alright, let's talk about two identical twin girls. I'll name one Isabella; care to name the other one?

AJ: How about… Sophia—after philosophy, of course.

Lucy: Ha! Nice choice, AJ. Okay, so we have Sophia and Isabella. But they are not really identical, even though they are called identical twins. Sophia is crawling on the floor, while at the same time Isabella is sleeping in her crib. If they were truly identical—one and the same—they couldn't perform contradictory actions such as sleeping and not sleeping at the same time.

AJ: Sure, but if there are two beings that are pure existence, they are not doing anything contradictory—they're just existing.

Lucy: Okay, but what makes them *two* distinct beings and not *one and the same* being? You have to point to at least one property that one has which the other does not.

AJ: Well, maybe one is thinking about humans and the other is thinking only about itself.

Lucy: So, you mean one of these beings *chose* to think about humans whereas the other being chose to think only about itself?

AJ: Yeah.

Lucy: But that would mean that both can change what they think about, which means both of these beings are a mixture of potentiality and actuality—and therefore neither is pure existence.

AJ: So, pure existence can't change.

Lucy: That's right.

AJ: And pure existence can't have any property—or anything whatsoever—that is distinct from its existence; otherwise, it would not be pure existence.

Lucy: Right, and that means that only one being can be pure existence.

AJ: Hmm… Well, you still have not given me a reason why I should believe that existence is more important than essence. And you still haven't shown why the unmoved mover of the first way and the uncaused cause of the second way are pure existence.

Lucy: Isn't it clear by now? Without existence, an essence is nothing. Dinosaurs are extinct; they no longer have existence. Anything that is a possible being is capable of existing and also capable of not existing because its essence is not identical to existence. Instead, it must receive existence from an external cause. This means that existence is related to essence as actuality to potentiality in a being whose existence is distinct from essence. For Aquinas, actuality, in its highest sense, is existence, which means there is an existential interpretation of the first way as well.[56]

AJ: How so?

Lucy: The first way reaches a pure actuality. Aristotle understood actuality as form, so he entertains the possibility of 47 or 55 unmoved movers.[57] But Aquinas understands actuality as existence, and therefore the pure actuality of the first way must be pure existence. Here is how he argues for that:

> Existence is that which makes every form or nature actual; for goodness and humanity are spoken of as actual, only because they are spoken of as existing. Therefore existence must be compared to essence, if the latter is a distinct reality, as actuality to potentiality. Therefore, since in God there is no potentiality … it follows that in Him essence does not differ from existence. Therefore His essence is His existence.[58]

And so the first and third ways both reach a cause that is pure existence.

AJ: And because there can only be one being that is pure existence, the first and third ways are talking about one and the same being—is that your point?

Lucy: Exactly!

AJ: And what about the uncaused cause of the second way?

Lucy: If there were a distinction between the existence and essence of the uncaused cause of the second way, it would be dependent on an external cause for its existence. Therefore, the only way for it to be truly uncaused is for its essence to be identical to its existence. So, the uncaused cause must also be pure existence.

AJ: And so the uncaused cause is referring to one and the same being as the first and third ways.

Lucy: Yes.

AJ: Okay, Lucy, I think you've got a point there. But I still have no idea what "pure existence" means and why we should call that God.

Lucy: That's a good question. But I'm not going to lie, I'm pretty tired and could use some sleep. How about we talk about that next time, after we discuss the fourth way?

AJ: Okay, fair enough. Get some sleep!

Lucy: Oh, I will!

Chapter 8

The Fourth Way: Argument from Degrees of Being

Lucy: Good morning, AJ.

AJ: Hi.

Lucy: You look as tired as I did yesterday—rough night?

AJ: More like a late night. You inspired me to read up on the fourth way. I have a whole bunch of objections.

Lucy: Wow. Look what I've done. You're becoming a philosopher, AJ. My secret plan is working....

AJ: Ha! *My* plan is to get some coffee. Give me a sec...

***

AJ: Okay, I'm ready. Would you mind if *I* read the fourth way?

Lucy: No, go ahead.

AJ: The fourth way is taken from the gradation to be found in things. Among beings there are some more and some less good, true, noble and the like. But "more" and "less" are predicated of different things, according as they resemble in their different ways something which is the maximum, as a thing is said to

69

be hotter according as it more nearly resembles that which is hottest; so that there is something which is truest, something best, something noblest and, consequently, something which is uttermost being; for those things that are greatest in truth are greatest in being, as it is written in Metaph. ii. Now the maximum in any genus is the cause of all in that genus; as fire, which is the maximum heat, is the cause of all hot things. Therefore there must also be something which is to all beings the cause of their being, goodness, and every other perfection; and this we call God.[59]

Now, Lucy, you have to admit that this is almost incomprehensible.

Lucy: Well, if it makes you feel any better, I do think it's the most difficult of the five ways.

AJ: No, it's worse than that. For example, what the heck does he mean when he says a thing is more or less true? *Things* are not true or false; *assertions* about things are true or false.

Lucy: Thomas is referring to true as a transcendental attribute of being.

AJ: Transcendental—what? I'm really beginning to think Thomas hides behind fancy language.

Lucy: AJ, I know this stuff is difficult, but either you make an effort to understand it or you quit—it's your choice. But you can't criticize it if you haven't made a good effort to understand it.

AJ: Well, I *can* criticize the presentation. Why didn't Thomas explain these five ways in greater depth? They are way too short, as far as I'm concerned.

Lucy: Actually, that's a fair point. But you have to remember they were written over seven hundred years ago for a different audience—young theologians, not skeptics and atheists.

AJ: And young theologians couldn't have benefited from more detail and explanation?

Lucy: Well, it seems, the *Summa theologiae* was meant to be taught by a Master teacher who would supplement the material and answer any questions.[60]

AJ: Alright, I guess it's hard to blame a guy in the 13th century for not writing for me in the 21st century.

Lucy: Right. So, Thomas is talking about the transcendental attributes of being. These are properties that every existing thing has in virtue of existing. In the case of truth, Thomas says truth primarily exists in an intellect.[61] For example, when I make the mental judgment that "AJ is drinking coffee," that judgment is true because it corresponds to how you are acting right now. You just spilled some, by the way.

AJ: My bad…continue.

Lucy: There are lots of other things that, potentially, you could be doing right now, but I can only know what activity you are *actually* doing. Your actions actualize my intellect, which means actuality is connected with knowledge of truth. But to act in some way is to exist in some way, and so actuality is connected with being. That's why a being *can* be called true—it's true in the sense that it's "knowable" by an intellect. And the more actuality a being has, the more knowable or true it is; and conversely, the truer something is, the greater it is in actuality and therefore in being.[62]

AJ: I'm not sure I understand all of that, but I have to say, Lucy, I'm impressed. You really *have* made an effort to understand this stuff.

Lucy: Thanks, I try. Listen, if you're having a hard time understanding being as true, I think I can explain the gist of the fourth way without it.

AJ: Please do.

Lucy: Okay. Let's focus on being as *good*. Thomas is saying that everything that exists is good in some way…

AJ: Hold up. Last week you said you believe in the reality of evil, right?

Lucy: Right.

AJ: But if evil exists, it can't be good. So, by your own admission, not everything that exists is good.

Lucy: No, you misunderstood me. When I said I believed in the reality of evil, I simply meant that it's true that people do evil things. People exist, and their actions exist, but evil in itself does not exist because evil is a lack of being.[63] It is similar to blindness in that a person can be blind, but while the person exists, the blindness does not exist because it is a *lack* of sight.

AJ: You mean like if you dig a hole in the ground, the dirt exists and the shovel exists, but the hole is just empty space—it's not a being. Is that what you mean?

Lucy: Right. Now, would you agree that at least some kinds of beings are better than others? It's better to be a human than a tree, right?

AJ: Maybe, but some trees live much longer than humans.

Lucy: Come on, AJ. Would you rather be a man or a tree?

AJ: Well, if I had to choose between being Adolf Hitler or a tree—I would choose a tree.

Lucy: Look, it's great that you don't want to be an evil man. But I think you're missing the point. Thomas isn't talking about individuals. He's talking about genera or *kinds* of being. That's why he also uses the word "noble." Some kinds of beings are better or nobler than others. It's better to be a plant than a stone, because a plant is alive, and it's better to be a human than a plant because humans are not only alive but also intelligent.[64]

AJ: Just curious, why is it good to be a stone?

Lucy: As Shakespeare would say, it's better to be than not to be. The alternative, *nothing*, is the absence of all goodness.

AJ: Okay, well, perhaps I just prefer being human because it has been wired into me to prefer my species over another by evolution.

Lucy: No, that would be something related to your personal or subjective feelings for humans. Thomas is using an *objective* notion of good to argue that humans are better than plants.

AJ: How does that argument go?

Lucy: Remember how earlier I said truth as a transcendental is related to the level of *knowability* of a being?

AJ: Yeah.

Lucy: Well, good is also a transcendental attribute of being, but it's related to the level of *perfection* of a being. The more perfect something is, the more we desire it, and the less perfect something is, the less we desire it.[65]

AJ: And perfect means…

Lucy: It means complete, not lacking anything. It comes from the Latin word *perfectus*, which is the past participle of the verb *perficere*, meaning to accomplish, finish, and complete.

AJ: You know Latin too?

Lucy: Not that well, but I've been studying it for two years so I can learn more about Thomas. Also, I have the *Online Etymology Dictionary* saved in my favorites.

AJ: Ha! And yet you're *still* single.

Lucy: Back to my point. We get an idea of a being's level of perfection by the kinds of actions it performs because perfection is related to actuality. When you were a child, AJ, you had a lot of potential because you were still growing and learning. But now you're better, because you're more fully developed.

AJ: Hmm… Taller, smarter, better looking…

Lucy: Sure. *Anyhow,* Thomas's point is that the more powerfully a thing can act, the more perfection it has, and…

AJ: …and the more actuality it has, the more being it has because to act in some way is to exist in some way?

Lucy: Correct. Now, it's a fact that humans can act in better ways than plants. For example, humans pursue science and invent technology, which shows that humans have more actuality than plants and thus are greater beings. You have to admit, your life would be much more limited and less perfect if you were a plant stuck in the ground, unable to walk, see, or reason.

AJ: Okay, it's true; I don't want to be a plant.

Lucy: Finally! Well, once you agree that some kinds of beings are better than others, you implicitly accept that there is a hierarchy or a ranking among beings. But more and less can only be predicated of different beings to the extent that they resemble something which is the maximum.

AJ: Alright, hold up. A few objections. For instance, Thomas gives the example of heat, saying, "A thing is said to be hotter according as it more nearly resembles that which is hottest," and then he adds, "Fire, which is the maximum heat, is the cause of all hot things."[66] This is just bad science, Lucy. How can you defend that?

Lucy: Granted, Thomas's example of heat and fire as the maximum of heat is bad; I can't defend it. But it's just an example. It doesn't mean his argument for a maximal being is bad.

AJ: Look at you agreeing with me that Thomas got something wrong.

Lucy: Sure. He's not infallible.

AJ: No, he certainly isn't. I can think of at least three other problems. First, Thomas appears to be treating being as a genus when he says, "The maximum in any genus is the cause of all in that genus …Therefore, there must also be something which is to all beings the cause of their being, goodness, and every other perfection; and this we call God."[67] But right after the five ways, Aquinas says God, who is Being Itself, is not in a genus:

> Since the existence of God is God's essence, as proven above, if God were to be in any genus, it would follow that God's genus would be being, for the genus signifies the essence of a thing, since it is predicated in its definition. But the Philosopher has shown in *Metaphysics* III that being cannot be anything's genus, for every genus has differences which are outside the essence of the genus; but no difference can possibly be found which would be outside of being, since nonbe-

ing cannot be a difference. Hence it follows that God is not in any genus.[68]

Told you I did my homework.

Lucy: Look at you! Admit it, as cool as science is, philosophy is a different kind of cool...

AJ: It's better than I thought, sure. So, what's your answer?

Lucy: Okay. In one of his earlier works, Thomas says anything that encompasses and contains many things, because it is common to them, can also be called a genus, though in a less proper sense.[69] Since stones, plants, and humans are all *beings*, being can be understood as a genus due to its commonness.

AJ: Fine, but there's a second problem. How can we know that a maximum or perfect being exists merely from observing a hierarchy of sensible things? It seems Thomas concludes too quickly to a maximum when he says, "There is something which is truest, something best, something noblest and, consequently, something which is uttermost being."[70] Dawkins makes a great point about this in *The God Delusion*. He says that if you say there must be an all-perfect being to make sense of the varying degrees of perfection, then, and I quote, "You might as well say, people vary in smelliness but we can make the comparison only by reference to a perfect maximum of conceivable smelliness. Therefore there must exist a pre-eminently peerless stinker."[71] But that's absurd.

Lucy: Alright, since you've opened this door, let me address the smelliness objection. Suppose you and some of your friends get together for an all-weekend long *Halo* tournament.

AJ: Such a good game!

Lucy: You play through the night, drinking Mountain Dew, eating Doritos. Eventually, even those who bothered to wear deodorant begin to smell. By the end of the weekend, don't you think you'd be able to pick out who generally smells the worst? You know, *that guy*?

AJ: That's definitely the *most* disgusting analogy you've used so far—I know that! But judging which smell is most offensive is subjective, Lucy. So, your example doesn't work.

Lucy: Alright, wouldn't someone at this *Halo* marathon be the tallest? That's certainly not subjective, right?

AJ: Okay, there's probably one person who is the tallest, but that's a *relative* maximum, not an absolute maximum. I can judge whether or not a man is taller than other men without having to believe that there exists somewhere a man of infinite height!

Lucy: That's true, but I don't think Thomas is arguing for an absolute maximum at that stage of the argument. In fact, the second sentence of the fourth way, which you read, can be translated as "But more and less are said of diverse things according as they *approach* in different ways to something which is most."[72]

AJ: Well, then, how does he argue for an absolute maximum being? Because if he can't, the fourth way fails.

Lucy: I think that comes near the end when he says, "Now the maximum in any genus is the cause of all in that genus ... Therefore there must also be something which is to all beings the cause of their being, goodness, and every other perfection; and this we call God."[73]

AJ: And that would be the third problem I have, Lucy—I think that principle is false.

Lucy: You mean that "the maximum in any genus is the cause of all in that genus"?

AJ: Yes, and I can prove it false. According to Thomas, human beings are the maximum in the genus of animal, right?

Lucy: Correct.

AJ: But clearly Thomas doesn't hold that humans are the cause of all the other species of animals, so the principle is false.

Lucy: That just shows the principle is sometimes false.

AJ: *Seriously*? Look, if there are doubts about the truth of a premise in an argument, then we can't conclude from that argument that the conclusion is true. Surely, you would not deny that?

Lucy: No, I wouldn't. But Thomas's principle must be true when these two conditions are met: (1) when the things in the genus require a cause, and (2) when it's impossible for the cause of the things in the genus to be outside of that genus.[74] Now, it's easy to see that condition two is true. Ask yourself, is it possible for a cause of things in the genus *being* to be outside of the genus being? The answer is no—for to "be" outside of the genus of being would mean to be non-being, or nothing, which can't act as a cause. So, all I have to do now is defend condition one by explaining why the gradations of limited beings we experience need a cause.

AJ: Alright, then explain why they need a cause—and explain why they can't just evolve from lower life-forms.

Lucy: I will. But, first, earlier you agreed there is a hierarchy of beings, that some kinds of beings are better than others, right?

AJ: Yes.

Lucy: But you would also admit that, although humans are better than plants and stones, humans are still not perfect in every way, right?

AJ: That's obvious.

Lucy: In fact, I bet you'd agree that nothing you have encountered or learned about is totally perfect in every way, correct?

AJ: Yes, I'd agree with that.

Lucy: Good. So, now I'm ready to argue why the gradations of limited beings we experience need a cause. This is going to get complicated.

AJ: Okay, you have my full attention.

Lucy: So, we begin with another thought experiment. If something's essence were identical to its existence, it would be pure existence, or if you prefer, Being Itself. It would also be pure actuality, for existence is what makes something actual. And it would be totally perfect because, as I explained earlier, perfection is linked to actuality. But none of the beings we experience in life are totally perfect, as you conceded. That means that something must be limiting their existence, namely, their essence or nature. Plants cannot walk or reason because their nature limits what they can do. So when a thing only possesses being in a limited way, such as a plant does, that means the thing in question had the potential to receive being but only to a degree. But something cannot actualize its own potential to receive being, for then it would cause its own existence, which is impossible. Therefore, a cause external to it must give it being. And it is for this reason that all things which possess being in a limited way require a cause.[75] With me so far?

AJ: I think so.

Lucy: Good. Now, the cause of all these things, which possess being in a limited way, cannot itself possess being in a limited way—otherwise it too would be dependent on a cause. So, the cause of the being of limited beings must be unlimited or maximal being—it must be existence itself, which is an absolute maximum. And if you remember from last time, I argued that there can be only one being that is existence itself—therefore, the first four ways are all talking about one and the same being, because they all conclude to something that is existence itself.

AJ: And evolution won't work because the less noble life-forms from which the others evolve are also limited beings that require a cause of their existence?

Lucy: Yes. Things have to exist before they can evolve, AJ. And the fourth way shows that limited beings must receive their existence from Maximal Being, or Being Itself. But that doesn't mean that evolution isn't part of God's plan; however, that's probably a topic for another time.

AJ: Well, there's one last promise you have to keep before you go.

Lucy: You mean when I promised last time that I'd explain what "pure existence" means and why we should call it God?

AJ: Yeah, because, to be honest, it's still very unclear to me.

Lucy: Well, in this life we don't experience God directly, so we can't know what Pure Existence is like. The five ways only give us an indirect knowledge of Pure Existence, because they argue from effects to a cause; and because these effects fall far short of their cause, we can't have perfect knowledge of God.[76]

AJ: So, what can we know about Pure Existence?

Lucy: Well, Pure Existence is complete perfection, lacking nothing. All of the perfections you see in the limited things around you, such as life and intelligence, must exist in God; otherwise, God could not cause these perfections in limited beings.

AJ: Wait a minute. That doesn't seem to make sense. Humans have the ability to see, which is a perfection—one that plants lack. But it's only because we have eyes that we can see. But God doesn't have eyes, right? So, God can't have all the perfections of limited things.

Lucy: True, God doesn't have physical eyes. But Thomas isn't saying that God has all the perfections of limited things *in the same way* that those limited things possess them. Instead, Thomas says that the perfections of all things preexist in God in an *eminent way*.[77] Sight gives us a kind of limited knowledge, but God possesses knowledge in a higher and perfect way. God's way of knowing includes whatever is good in the power of sight but transcends it.[78]

AJ: And because God transcends human nature, we can't know much about Pure Existence.

Lucy: That's right. Perhaps the best we can do is to examine our own existence, AJ. After all, you and I exist, but with limitations and imperfections. Try to imagine how it would be to exist without your limitations, and you'll get a glimpse of what it would be like to be Pure Existence. For example, imagine yourself as a mind existing without a body. You wouldn't require food or sleep. Now try to fully remove the limitations of space. Imagine you are present everywhere in the universe, instead of being limited to a small region of space on the planet earth. Now, try to remove the limitations of time. As an eternal being you would know all things at once. What humans call the past, present, and future would all be a single eternal moment for you. You would know all things, and not because those things cause a change in you, as when you drink coffee, but because you are the cause of them. Imagining these things is difficult, but it gives us a glimpse of the majesty and complete perfection of Pure Existence and why it's worthy of the name God. It also happens to be the name God gave to Moses in the book of Exodus: "I am the God who IS."[79]

AJ: Hmm… I'm still trying to imagine what it would be like to exist without any limitations—mind-bending stuff, Lucy!

Lucy: See you tomorrow?

AJ: Definitely.

Chapter 9

The Fifth Way:
Argument from Finality

AJ: Hey, good morning! I think this is the first time I've arrived before you. I got you a coffee.

Lucy: Thanks so much. Look at you with your notes out and all ready to go.

AJ: Ha! What can I say? I love arguing about the big things. Want me to read the fifth way?

Lucy: Actually, would you mind if I read it? I'll explain why in a second.

AJ: Sure.

Lucy: Okay.

> The fifth way is taken from the governance of the world. We see that things which lack intelligence, such as natural bodies, act for an end, and this is evident from their acting always, or nearly always, in the same way, so as to obtain the best result. From this it is obvious that they achieve their end not by chance but by natural inclination. Now whatever lacks intelligence cannot move towards an end, unless it be directed by some being endowed with knowledge and intelligence; as the arrow is shot

to its mark by the archer. Therefore some intelligent being exists by whom all natural things are directed to their end; and this being we call God.[80]

AJ: Wait, is that a different translation or something?

Lucy: It is.

AJ: You changed the part ... hold on a sec ... okay, here it is: "Hence it is plain that not fortuitously, but designedly, do they achieve their end."

Lucy: Wow, you've had your coffee this morning! You're right, I think what I read is a better translation.

AJ: Why?

Lucy: Before I can explain that, we need to understand the argument. How would you summarize it?

AJ: Okay, I'd say that everything we see appears as if it were designed to act for a goal. Seeds grow into flowers, never chickens. Bees collect nectar from flowers to make honey and to help flowers reproduce. Thomas wants to say that the only explanation for this appearance of design is that there is a God directing it all. But surely evolution has done away with this argument, which may have sounded plausible in the 13th century when Aquinas lived.[81]

Lucy: Still relying on Dawkins, I see.

AJ: Why not? He's a biologist, unlike Aquinas.

Lucy: That's true, but the fifth way isn't only about living beings. Many atheists misunderstand this point. They seem to think that if evolution is true, then the argument fails.

AJ: That's kinda what I was thinking, too.

Lucy: I can see why you'd think that, since Thomas's argument isn't very long. But actually, Thomas isn't talking only about living beings; he's talking about non-living things—such as stones and fire—as well. In his conclusion he says, "All *natural* things are directed to their end."

AJ: Stones and fire?

Lucy: Yeah, Thomas didn't know about modern physics, obviously; he thought that heavy objects, such as stones, have a natural inclination to fall, and conversely, that light objects, such as fire, have a natural inclination to rise.[82] His examples aren't the best, granted, but his general point is sound.

AJ: How is it sound?

Lucy: Well, I mean, scientists have discovered that many non-living things act for an end. For example, electrons, by nature, are attracted to protons. If electrons didn't have this natural inclination, then none of the elements on the periodic table you studied in Chemistry would form, which means none of the physical life forms you experience—including yourself— would exist anywhere in the physical universe. So, evolution wouldn't even be possible if the building blocks of the universe did not have the right kinds of natural inclinations.

AJ: Is that why you translated that sentence as "it is obvious that they achieve their end not by chance but by natural inclination" instead of "not fortuitously, but designedly"?

Lucy: Yes, and let me explain this more thoroughly, as I promised earlier. Thomas begins by talking about things that lack intelligence but which routinely act for a goal that is good. Since they lack intelligence they can't choose to act in that way. And because they routinely act in that way, we can rule out chance as the explanation.

AJ: Because things that happen by chance only happen rarely.

Lucy: That's right. So, the only other explanation that makes sense is to say that electrons act this way because of a natural inclination they have. The Latin that was translated as 'designedly' in the fifth way is *ex intentione*, which, in other passages, Thomas identifies with the natural inclinations of non-intelligent things.[83]

AJ: Is natural inclination the only other explanation? It sounds to me like Aquinas is saying—or would say—that God moves the electron to the proton. He even gives the example of an arrow being shot to its destination by an archer.

Lucy: I thought you might be interpreting it that way. But, no, that's not correct. Each of the five ways begins with things we know about the world through our senses. Thomas specifically begins the fifth way with our knowledge of non-intelligent, natural bodies routinely acting for a goal that is good. But if God is moving everything like a Puppeteer, then the fifth way wouldn't begin with the *natural actions* of natural bodies.[84] Plus, I don't think it's possible to know with our *senses* that God is moving everything like a Puppeteer—and if we *could* know that through our senses, then we wouldn't need a rational argument to prove God's existence.

AJ: Well, technically, we don't know that electrons are attracted to protons through our senses.

Lucy: You're right. But it *is* a fact discovered by science. Besides, we don't know about evolution through our senses either—that's why it took so long to discover. So, if you're going to use discoveries in biology to try to argue against the fifth way, I can appeal to discoveries in physics to argue for the fifth way. The principle of charity in philosophy requires that we consider the best and strongest interpretation of Aquinas's argument—something some critics fail to do.

AJ: Fair enough. But if an electron has a natural inclination to be attracted to the proton, then why do we need God? Why not prefer the simpler explanation? Why violate Ockham's razor and posit some supernatural being?

Lucy: We need to posit an intelligent cause because if we don't, we can't explain why the electron *has* the natural inclination it does to routinely act for an end that is good.

AJ: But maybe it's just a brute fact that electrons have this inclination.

Lucy: Do you remember in *The God Delusion*, when Dawkins mentions that a "sophisticated heat seeking missile" is a better example than Aquinas's example of the arrow?[85]

AJ: Sure.

Lucy: Well, Dawkins was right about that.

AJ: Mind if I record you saying that?

Lucy: Let me explain why. In the case of the arrow, its movement to the target is totally dependent on the archer. If the archer does not place the arrow on the bow, aim, and release the arrow, it can't hit the target. So, although we need intelligence to explain how and why the arrow keeps hitting the target, the inclination to the target isn't within the arrow itself. Instead, hitting the target is imposed on the arrow by an external cause, the archer. But a heat-seeking missile, unlike the arrow, has the ability to change course on its own in the middle of flight. This is because it can track infrared light emission and follow it wherever it moves. So, the heat-seeking missile possesses an inclination to its target that more closely resembles the inclination of an electron to a proton.

AJ: So, let me guess. Your point is that the missile, being non-intelligent, could never have given itself this inclination. Instead, a human engineer had to give this inclination to the missile. Is that right?

Lucy: Exactly. There are two levels of causality that must exist in order for the heat-seeking missile to act in the way it does. First, there's the physical level of causality—its circuitry and heat sensors, etc.—all of which work together and are internal to the missile itself. Second, there's the intelligent level of causality, which comes from the engineer, who is external to the missile, but who is responsible for designing the missile so it can act on its own in a specific way.

AJ: That's certainly true of human inventions, but I don't see why it has to be true about the universe. Why can't the electron just have this inclination as a brute fact? Maybe that's just the way the universe is. I don't get why we have to appeal to an intelligent cause.

Lucy: Because an intelligent level of causality is necessary to explain anything that routinely acts for an end that is good. Let me read to you how Thomas explains it:

> Those things that are possessed of reason move themselves to an end; because they have dominion over their actions through their free-will, which is the faculty of will and reason. But those things that lack reason tend to an end, by natural inclination, as

being moved by another and not by themselves; *since they do not know the nature of an end as such*, and *consequently cannot ordain anything to an end, but can be ordained to an end only by another....* Consequently it is proper to the rational nature to tend to an end, as directing and leading itself to the end: whereas it is proper to the irrational nature to tend to an end, *as directed or led by another*, whether it apprehends the end, as do irrational animals, or does not apprehend it, as is the case of those things which altogether lack knowledge.[86]

AJ: I get that an electron lacks intelligence and free-will, so it can't choose to move to the proton, but I still don't get why the goal of an electron has to be ordained by an agent.

Lucy: Alright, let me try something else. Suppose I were to reach out and hold your hand.

AJ: Okay…

Lucy: It's just a thought experiment, AJ.

AJ: Sure, please continue.

Lucy: That would be an example of me acting for an end. And in order to hold hands, I have to move closer to you—that's an example of me ordering a means to an end. Aristotle and Aquinas call the end or goal the *final cause*, which in this case is holding your hand. And there is a relationship between the final cause and the efficient cause, which in this case is me, because I'm the one reaching out to hold your hand.

AJ: Okay, I'm with you.

Lucy: Good, because the relationship between the final cause and the efficient cause is really important. A goal is pursued because it's desirable or good in some way, and so the final cause explains why something has acted for an end. But the final cause or goal in this case, which is holding hands, can only influence me to perform an action if it is somehow present in me now, at this very moment. But holding hands, which is a physical act, doesn't exist now. So, how can it influence my action?

AJ: Because you're thinking about it?

Lucy: Exactly. Because I'm intelligent, I can envision something mentally that does not yet exist physically, and I can deliberate about which means to the end will most effectively bring about that end. This is only possible because my intellect is non-material, which allows me to think freely and abstractly about a material future that could exist but that does not exist now. However, a material thing, such as an electron, is incapable of acting freely, of thinking abstractly about the future, and of having knowledge of any kind—and thus it's confined only to the here and now.[87] It can't establish for itself any kind of relation to an end. So, if an electron has a natural inclination to something outside itself—the proton—an end it could neither have known about nor have established, then that inclination must have been caused in it by an intelligent cause exterior to it.

AJ: How can you determine that the electron's inclination to the proton is good? It's not so clear what good means in that case. Is the electron desiring the proton? That sounds silly. It's probably easier for Aquinas to discuss animals, which act to obtain food or to protect themselves, as those are easier to understand as being good for the animal. But, of course, I think evolution is a better explanation for that kind of activity.

Lucy: I agree it's easier to judge the goodness of the ends of living beings, especially when they clearly act for self-preservation. But I'm trying to focus on the part of Aquinas's fifth way that's not affected by evolution.[88] And, as I mentioned earlier, if electrons didn't have a natural inclination to protons, then none of the elements on the periodic table would form and therefore no physical life forms would exist anywhere in the physical universe. If you agree that life, including your own life, is good, then it's hard to see the natural inclination of the electron to the proton as anything other than good.

AJ: Maybe. But there's something else bothering me. You're saying that there's an Intelligence that has designed the electron to be attracted to the proton and which has designed the proton to attract the electron. But this sounds a lot like the Watchmaker God of William Paley.[89] But how do we know this Grand Engineer isn't some super-advanced alien being, or a whole species of them!?

Lucy: How could an alien who is part of the universe be responsible for the direction and governance of the universe as a whole?

AJ: Okay, fine. All I'm saying is that it doesn't prove the existence of a Creator. And that's what you need to prove if you want people to believe in your God.

Lucy: I want to address your comments about the Watchmaker God of Paley, because it's a common misunderstanding of Thomas's fifth way.

AJ: I'm listening.

Lucy: First, Paley lived during a time when many viewed the world mechanically, as if it were a Big Clock.[90] Second, Paley limits his argument to complex things in nature that have parts, such as the human eye.[91] He says that *mechanism*s exist in animals, which resemble machines made by human art; and it is from such mechanisms in nature that he argues to God.[92] But when you focus on mechanisms, it's easy to view God as similar to an engineer who imposes activity on something—that's what we call *extrinsic finality*. For example, a piece of metal, by its nature, doesn't tell time. However, an engineer can arrange metal into springs, gears, and so on, and force it to do something that's contrary to its nature—to tell time.

AJ: But Thomas uses the analogy of the archer, who you said imposes activity on the arrow.

Lucy: I know, but you have to let me finish.

AJ: Okay.

Lucy: Thomas is clear in other passages that God uses *intrinsic finality*—in other words, God gives things their own causal power and natural inclinations so they can act on their own level of causality. Let me read one of these passages to you:

> The natural necessity inherent in those beings which are determined to a particular thing, is a kind of impression from God, directing them to their end; as the necessity whereby an arrow is moved so as to fly towards a certain point is an impression from the archer, and not from the arrow. But there is a difference, inasmuch as that which creatures receive from God is their nature [intrinsic finality], while that which natural things receive from man in addition to their nature [extrinsic finality] is somewhat violent. Wherefore, as the violent necessity in the movement of the arrow shows the action of the archer, so the

natural necessity of things shows the government of Divine Providence.[93]

AJ: I assume by "violent" Thomas means something that's contrary to its nature.

Lucy: Correct. It's not in the nature of wood, which is the natural substance from which arrows are made, to fly through the air and hit targets.

AJ: I got it. But I'm confused about something. When we discussed the second way, you said that God helped you, Lucy, to move the book that you were pushing with your hand. But now, you're saying things can act on their own. Which is it?

Lucy: You have to think of *two* levels of causality working together. Think back to the analogy of driving the car that I gave you when we discussed the second way. You can turn the steering wheel and drive where you choose— that's the analogy to the human level of causality. But you can't drive any-more if you run out of gas—that's the analogy to God's level of causality. So, I have some power to act on my level of causality, but I'm still continu-ally dependent on God's level of causality in order to exist and act.[94]

AJ: Alright, putting that aside, is your point that a Watchmaker God uses only extrinsic finality, so He can't be the kind of God that Aquinas is talking about?

Lucy: That's right. To understand the fifth way correctly requires under-standing that Aquinas is using the intrinsic finality of non-intelligent beings to demonstrate the existence of God. God is the ultimate cause of why such beings act routinely for an end that is good, because God is the cause of why these beings have natural inclinations. God can give them these natural inclinations because He is intelligent. But God doesn't do this like a human engineer, who imposes an end on an already existing thing. Instead, God is the cause of *why these things exist and have the natures and natural inclinations that they do.* Only a cause that is Being Itself can impart being and natural inclinations to things.

AJ: You mean God creates things that didn't exist before.

Lucy: Yes. All of the five ways conclude to one and the same cause, which is Being Itself. This lays the foundation for the argument that God alone can create or bring things into being from nothing—that is, from no pre-existing thing.[95]

AJ: That sounds like creationism to me. I don't really see how this is compatible with evolution.

Lucy: Things have to exist before they can evolve. Plus, as I mentioned earlier, the basic building blocks of the universe have to have the right natures and inclinations for life and evolution to be possible. There is no incompatibility between God and evolution because God can make things so that they have the power to evolve. In fact, Aquinas argues that God's goodness is so great that He made things not only to exist but also so that they could be causes for other things.[96]

AJ: So, you're saying God could create the world in such a way that evolution would happen, which means evolution would be part of God's plan...

Lucy: Sure, why not?

AJ: Well, let me ask you this. Does God have to intervene in the course of evolution to get what he wants? If so, that sounds a lot like those intelligent design people, who say that evolution couldn't produce the flagellum of bacteria; therefore, God had to do it.

Lucy: You're talking about Michael Behe. But Thomas's argument in the fifth way is *not* the same as Behe's argument about the flagellum. Behe's argument is that the tail or flagellum of bacteria is very complex, almost like an outboard motor of a boat. In fact, he argues that the flagellum is irreducibly complex, such that if you remove any of the parts it won't function; thus, it had to be produced all at once, and not incrementally through evolution.[97]

AJ: That sounds like the God-of-the-gaps fallacy to me.

Lucy: It is.

AJ: It is?

Lucy: That's right, I'm agreeing with you. Behe's argument isn't the same as Aquinas's argument in the fifth way.

AJ: You mean that if Aquinas were alive today he would say that evolution can produce the flagellum?

Lucy: I think so. Remember, Thomas believes in different levels of causality that work together without gaps. Let me give you another analogy to explain what I mean. Imagine that in the future houses are built by robots. The architect uploads the plans to the head robot, provides the robots with wood, nails, and other materials, and then goes away on vacation for two weeks. Upon returning, the architect finds that the robots have finished building the house—it's even painted!

AJ: Your point is?

Lucy: Even though the robot's level of causality is seamless—there are no gaps where the architect had to step in and help the robots build the house—we still need another level of causality, besides the robots, to explain the existence of the house.

AJ: You mean the plans or blueprint made by the architect?

Lucy: Exactly. The architect represents the intelligent level of causality that is necessary for the robots to build the house. These two levels of causality peacefully co-exist—they are not in competition—and neither level has any gaps. But while the robots act as *assembler causes*, they are different from, but dependent upon, the cause responsible for the *plan* of the house.[98]

AJ: Okay, I get it. You're saying God creates the world in such a way that evolution can assemble the flagellum of bacteria, but only because God gave the right causal powers and inclinations to natural things.

Lucy: Yep, you got it.

AJ: Yeah ... But I don't know if it's true, Lucy. It's a lot to think about.

Lucy: I understand.

AJ: Same time tomorrow?

Lucy: No, I...

AJ: No? But, I was hoping we could continue our discussion about...

Lucy: No, you don't understand. I'm leaving tonight.

AJ: Leaving?

Lucy: I'm flying to Poland. I'm going to a philosophy conference.

AJ: Well, what's this conference about?

Lucy: It's about the epistemology of finding God.

AJ: What?

Lucy: The different ways we can come to know of God—you know the philosophical proofs, faith, and mystical experience. I'm going to give a presentation about how I found God through prayer.

AJ: It wasn't through Aquinas?

Lucy: No, that came later.

AJ: How long will you be gone? Can I drop you off at the airport?

Lucy: Ten days. My mother has a friend in Lublin, whom I'll be staying with. And, thanks, but my Dad's dropping me off.

AJ: Okay. Well, I mean, thanks so much for taking the time to answer all my questions—even if I didn't agree with all of your answers. You know, I really appreciate…

Lucy: AJ, I'm just going to Poland. I'm coming back … You know what? My flight isn't till 11 p.m., and I hate airplane food. How about we catch a quick dinner later tonight, and I can tell you about my conference paper? Plus, I'd like to hear your comments on it. I have to warn you though: it's the story about how I found Christ.

AJ: Sure. I'd love to. I'm not saying I'll be convinced; in fact, I'm almost certain I won't be. But I'd be interested in hearing about it.

Lucy: Great. I have to go home now and finish packing, but I'll see you later…

AJ: Wait. Where am I… How am I going to meet you? And what time?

Lucy: Here's my number. Text me.

AJ: I will.

Lucy: I know.

Part II

ADDITIONAL RESOURCES

Chapter 10
Philosophical Terms and Concepts[99]

Whether you're in the middle of reading the dialogue of AJ and Lucy and want more clarification of some terms or concepts, or you've finished the dialogue but want a deeper understanding of Aquinas so you can read more of him on your own, this chapter is for you.

The following terms and concepts are discussed below in the order they are listed here, so they'll be easy to find. Just look for these boldface headings:

1. Being and Essence

2. Substance and Accident

3. Necessary and Possible Being

4. Substantial and Accidental Change

5. Potentiality and Actuality

6. Linear and Hierarchical Causal Series

7. Four Causes and Five Ways

8. The Structure of the Five Ways

9. Reasoning to God's Existence (And Why God Cannot Be Defined)

Note: You can skip right to the section you want to learn more about.

But if you have more time, it's probably a good idea to read this entire chapter from beginning to end. This is because the order in which these terms and concepts are discussed is important. Later terms and concepts build off of earlier ones. For example, to really understand substantial and accidental change, you need to understand what a substance and an accident are. But don't worry; we've made it fun and easy.

1. Being and Essence

You can't read Aquinas without coming across the term "being." Of course, all of us use that word in everyday language. We talk about human *beings,* or, *being* unable to understand Aquinas!

For Aquinas, anything that exists is a being. You, the person reading this book, are a being. The stone you pick up at the beach is a being, and so is the rainbow you see in the sky. Even the dream you had last night can be called a being, because it *existed* in your mind. But humans, stones, rainbows, and dreams are different *kinds* of beings, which leads us to another important philosophical term: "essence."

"Essence" refers to *what* a being is.[100] You, the reader of this book, are *human.* That is your essence. For our purposes in this book, "essence" can also be called "nature." The traditional definition of human is *rational animal.* When you understand what a rational animal is, then you understand human nature or essence. Animal is the genus, or general category, to which humans belong. As animals, humans are material, living, and sentient beings. But what, traditionally, separates the human species from other species of animal is that humans have the power of reason or intelligence.

Essence determines what kind of being something is—for example, *human* as opposed to *feline* or *canine.* Therefore, essence limits existence. To be a human—a rational animal—carries with it many limitations. Humans cannot fly in the air like birds, or breathe underwater, like fish. The essence of a thing also determines whether or not it is the *kind* of thing that can exist on its own or must exist in something else. This leads to our next set of important philosophical terms: "substance" and "accident."

2. Substance and Accident

Suppose, for instance, you meet a person named Mary, who is five feet tall, knows (and teaches) biology, and is the mother of one child. The property of being five feet tall, which we call a *quantity*, can only exist *in* a material being. Similarly, *knowledge* of biology, which is a *quality*, can only exist *in* an intelligent being. Finally, *being a mother*, which is a relation, only exists for as long as both Mary and her child exist. This is because the relation of *being a mother* has a foundation *in* two beings.

Quantities, qualities, and relations, though different, are collectively referred to as "accidents." The essence of an accident—that is, the kind of thing an accident is—is something that must exist *in* something else. In contrast, it belongs to the essence of a substance *not to exist in something else, but by itself.*[101] So, *human*, which expresses Mary's essence, is a substance because it is the kind of thing to which it belongs not to exist in something else, but by itself. Cat is another example of a substance, and so is the metal Gold.

While Human, Cat, and Gold are *kinds* of substances, an individual person, such as Mary, is an example of what we call a primary substance. Mary is a primary substance because she is an *actually existing human being*, in which accidents, such as knowledge and being five feet tall, exist. Mary has what Aquinas calls *real existence*, which is existence in the world that exists outside of our minds—the world of mountains, trees, and other people. In contrast, a dream we have during the night only has *cognitional* or *mental existence*, for it only exists in our mind.

Without real existence we can only think or talk about a substance (or essence) in an abstract way—that is, to the extent we can understand it in our mind. For example, Tyrannosaurus Rex is a kind of substance—a large, bipedal, carnivorous dinosaur. But this is an example of an essence that does not have real existence. Although we have some understanding of its essence from studying its fossils, these dinosaurs no longer exist and have been extinct for millions of years.

So, to sum up, *this* human (Mary) or *this* cat (Fluffy) refers to a primary substance, whereas *Cat* or *Human* is what we call "secondary substance," which is related to the essence of a thing. While it might be tempting to think that God is the *most* primary substance of them all, that would be incorrect. God is not a primary substance.[102] This is because a substance always refers to some kind of *essence*, such as Human or Cat, to which it belongs not to exist in something else, but by itself.[103] However, after the five ways, Aquinas argues that God does not have an essence that limits His Being.[104] Instead, he argues, God's existence is identical to His essence.[105] This leads to an important distinction between "necessary being" and "possible being."

3. Necessary and Possible Being

The description Aquinas uses to refer to God is "Subsistent Being Itself" (*Ipsum Esse Subsistens*).[106] Let's examine this description more closely, but keep in mind that sometimes in this book we will shorten it to "Being Itself" for convenience.

God is appropriately called *Being* because, as mentioned earlier, anything that exists is a being. But unlike Mary, whose human essence limits her being, God does not have an essence that limits His being. This means that God is *Being Itself*, not *human* being, or *feline* being. Finally, we use the term "subsistent" to describe a being that is capable of existing, not in another, but by itself. Because Being Itself does not exist *in* anything else, God is subsistent, which completes the description "Subsistent Being Itself."

If Aquinas is correct that God is Subsistent Being Itself, then God exists *necessarily*. In other words, God is Necessary Being, which means it is impossible for God not to exist. There are two reasons for this. First, as Being Itself, God does not require a cause to give Him being because *He is Being*. Second, as Being Itself, God does not have an essence that can lose its existence, as in the case of the essence Tyrannosaurs Rex, which no longer has real existence.

When it is possible for a being to exist or not exist, Aquinas calls it a possible being. Possible beings are also called contingent beings, because their existence is dependent on a cause. Indeed, Aquinas argues to God's existence through the contingent existence of possible beings in the third way. And one way we become aware of contingent existence is through the fact that primary substances undergo different kinds of change. Let's consider that next.

4. Substantial and Accidental Change

Over time, a primary substance, such as Mary, will undergo change. Some of these changes will be in quantity, quality, and relation, and therefore they are called *accidental changes*. For example, growing in height, learning something new, and becoming a mother are all accidental changes. These kinds of changes make Mary exist in a new way but do not change Mary's essence, for Mary remains a human being throughout all of them. However, Aquinas argues that a cause external to Mary is required to explain how she exists in a new way when she acquires a new accidental property.

105

Not all changes are accidental, however. Some kinds of changes are substantial, as when Mary dies, for example. Mary is a rational animal—a living substance—but upon death her bodily remains are no longer a living substance. Another example of a substantial change would be when scientists convert one substance, such as bismuth (a metallic element next to lead on the periodic table), into a different substance, such as gold. This can (and has been) done in particle accelerators.[107] Because gold and bismuth are different with respect to essence, this is an example of a substantial change. Maybe we owe the alchemists an apology...

Substantial changes also require causes to explain the new substantial existence that is acquired after the change has taken place. For example, a new human being comes into existence when sperm and egg join and undergo a substantial change. We use the term "generation" to signify the new substance that is coming into existence, and the term "corruption" to signify the old substance or substances that are passing out of existence. Aquinas argues that the fact that a thing is generated—such as you from your parents—tells us something, indirectly, about your existence—that it is contingent. Indeed, anything that undergoes a substantial change—that comes into existence or passes out of existence—is a contingent being.

Substantial and accidental changes are only possible because primary substances have the potential to change, which leads us to another set of important philosophical terms: "potentiality" and "actuality."

5. Potentiality and Actuality

When Aquinas uses the word "motion," he means more than an object moving in space. He uses the word "motion" to describe any kind of change. When your fingernails grow, that's motion. When water freezes into ice, that's motion. When your hair is lightened by the sun (or hair dye!), that's motion.

Within this definition of motion, we find the concepts of potentiality and actuality (also called potency and act). Something in motion is in the process of being reduced from potentiality to actuality.[108] Actuality is what the being currently possesses. Potentiality is the ability of the being to become something else. For example, if I am dyeing my hair from blond to brown, in actuality it is blond. It has the potentiality to become brown, but it is not brown yet. The process of dyeing my hair is the process in which my hair's potential for brownness becomes actual; my hair is moved from potentially brown to actually brown.

Most of us would no doubt agree that motion is a very common process in the world, and movement is caused by a mover. But we should ask ourselves, "Have I ever seen something move or change itself, or have I only seen things whose change was caused by something outside themselves?" When your hair lightens, it does so because of the sun or hair dye. When water becomes ice, it does so because of the cold temperature. These things are moved from potentiality to actuality by something outside of themselves.

Those examples are pretty obvious, though. Let's take a look at something less obvious—the free actions of human beings. It seems that humans are capable of moving themselves when they act freely. After all, how can my action be free if I am moved by another? Aquinas does not deny human freedom, and he agrees that there is a sense in which you can say humans are self-moved. However, his point is that humans are not *entirely* self-moved. The reason is that no being can be (at the same time) in a state of actuality and potentiality with respect to the same thing. For example, suppose I decide to study the Chinese language. First, I have to know it exists before I can choose to study it. There was a time as a child when I didn't know about the Chinese language at all, but I had the potential to learn about it. It was only after I heard Chinese that this potential was actualized by another (the person speaking Chinese). Only after this actualization of my potentiality could I then choose to study the Chinese language. At that point, I knew Chinese existed but I did not understand the words and grammar of the language. I had the potential to learn the words and grammar, but I could not actualize this potential all by myself—for no being can be (at the same time) in a state of actuality and potentiality with respect to the same thing. Therefore, to learn Chinese I must be moved by another—a teacher who actually knows Chinese. It is because humans cannot actualize their potential all by themselves—but rather only with assistance from external causes—that humans are not entirely self-moved.

Because, as Aquinas argues, all things (except for God) have potentiality, ultimately, all things are dependent on God to actualize them. And, although it might seem paradoxical, God actualizes humans in such a way as to make human free choice possible. Here is an analogy: You can drive a car anywhere you choose, but you cannot drive at all without gasoline (or some kind of energy source). Similarly, God supplies you with the "energy" (the actuality) that you need to make a choice, but He leaves it up to you to choose what you want. So, even in the case of free human acts, humans are moved by another (God) but in a way that makes free action possible.

God does not need to be moved by another because, as Aquinas argues, God is pure actuality. God does not change but rather causes other things to change. As the unmoved mover, God has no unrealized potential. If ever we admit that a being has potential, then we know that being is not God. We must keep tracing the causes further until we do finally get to that one last mover. That one last mover—the unmoved mover—is pure actuality, having no potential and lacking nothing; that one last mover is the being for whom existence and essence are identical.[109] That being—and only that being—is the one that we can call God.

6. Linear and Hierarchical Causal Series

The examples given above, about learning Chinese and dyeing one's hair, are series of causes that are linear. In this type of series, one independent object interacts with another independent object and causes it to move, similar to a series of dominos. These changes take place over a period of time, whether short or long. Dye, for example, is applied to hair, and after a few minutes it changes color.

The examples of causal series just mentioned are also accidental, because the thing that has been moved is not continually dependent on its mover. For example, once I learn how to speak Chinese I can continue to speak it even if I never see the teacher who taught me Chinese again. Similarly, once my hair has changed color—because of the application of hair dye—my hair will not immediately revert to its old color when I throw out or destroy the remaining hair dye and applicator.

But there is a different kind of causal series, called an essential or hierarchical one, which is very important for our understanding of God. This kind of series is one in which the thing moved is continually dependent on the mover. In fact, every member of an essential causal series is dependent on each and every cause prior to it. Imagine, for example, that you see Thomas Aquinas's great works sitting on a table. These books are able to be positioned as they are because there is a table underneath them. In turn, the table is able to hold the books because it is supported by the floor. The floor rests on a foundation that lies on the earth. Everything in the series is essential to the end result: the book sitting on the table. If you took away the table, the book would not be sitting on it. And if the house no longer had a foundation, then the floor, the table, and even the books would ultimately collapse.

Examining a hierarchical series helps us to see God as the First Mover. When we consider a series of causes that all exist at the same time, we immediately recognize that something holds the series together. The table holds the book, the floor holds the table, the foundation holds the floor, and the earth holds the foundation. But, who holds the earth? Gravity, we might answer. But, what keeps gravity in existence? Eventually, in every hierarchical series, we trace the causes back to a first cause, a power that supports and holds everything together in existence. That power is God.

7. Four Causes and Five Ways

Because there are different kinds of causes, there will be different ways of establishing that God exists. Aquinas was influenced by Aristotle, who discussed four different kinds of causes: material, formal, efficient, and final.[110] Each of the five ways involves one or more of these causes, so a short explanation of them will be helpful.

The easiest way to understand the four causes is to think of a Sculptor producing a statue. The material cause is the stuff out of which the statue is made. Statues can be made out of different kinds of material—wood or metal, for instance. But let's go for the classic ancient Roman statue, which would be made out of marble.

The formal cause is that which makes it the kind of statue it is. When you look at a statue, usually you can tell fairly quickly whether it is a statue of a lion or human being or something else. It is the shape of the statue that tells you what it is a statue of, so in this case the shape is the formal cause. Usually, however, the formal cause will not be the shape of a thing. It is in this case because a statue is a human artifact, which is made to embody a shape.[111] A block of marble without a shape is not a statue. However, different natural substances, such as gold and lead, can have the same shape when made into coins, for example, but they are not the same kind of substance. Gold is an excellent conductor of electricity; lead is not. So, it is not the shape that makes gold and lead different substances. Neither does matter (the material cause) make them different kinds of substance. Both gold and lead are *material* substances; thus, being material is something they share in common. What accounts for the difference between gold and lead is that they have different *formal* causes.

The formal cause is something intrinsic to an individual substance and gives that substance its necessary properties. In the case of living things, Aristotle had a special name for the formal cause: the soul.[112] A piece of gold and a dog are both material substances, but the dog is alive, while the gold is not. It is the soul, which is internal to the dog, that accounts for why dogs are living substances. A carcass on the side of the road is not alive precisely because it does not have a soul.

Although it might be tempting to identify the formal cause with essence, Aquinas argues that the full essence of a material substance must take into account both the formal and the material causes.[113] This is because, in the case of material substances, neither the material cause nor the formal cause by itself is a complete substance. Only together do they make a complete substance.[114] However, when considering the relationship between these two kinds of causes, the formal cause is the active and primary cause responsible for making something to be the kind of substance it is, whereas the material cause is the passive and secondary cause. In this way, we can say that *form is actuality* and *matter is potentiality*, as discussed above.

Returning to our example of the statue, the efficient cause is what is primarily responsible for producing the statue. The marble changes into a statue because the sculptor hammers and chisels a shape into the marble. Now, although it is the chisel that actually touches the marble and removes stone, the chisel is merely an instrumental cause, which is incapable of any causal power without the sculptor to wield it. Aquinas, in his *Commentary on Aristotle's Physics*, describes the efficient cause as "that from which there is a beginning of motion or rest."[115] Clearly, then, it is the person who initiates the act of sculpting. While it is true to some extent to say that the human person chiseling the marble is the efficient cause, Aristotle counsels us to be more precise.[116] Not every human being knows how to sculpt a statue out of marble with a hammer and chisel. Only those humans who possess the art of sculpting, which is a kind of knowledge, are able to do so. But the art of sculpting only exists in a person, so the most precise answer is that the *sculptor* (the person possessing the art) is the efficient cause.

The final cause is that for the sake of which all was done. It is the aim or the goal of the process. In this case, the final cause is the statue itself. The final cause guided the process from start to finish, exerting influence over the material, formal, and efficient causes. For example, marble was chosen because it is a good material out of which to make a statue—whereas pudding would have been a poor choice for a statue. And some kind of shape had to be selected and put into the marble, because an uncarved piece of marble by itself is not a statue. The sculptor is the efficient cause. Lastly, the statue itself, which is the goal of the art of sculpting, is the final cause. Thus all four causes are necessary to give a general explanation of how statues are produced.

8. The Structure of the Five Ways

As mentioned earlier, each of the five ways involves one or more of the four causes. The general structure of each way is to highlight something a thing possesses that it could not have given itself and therefore that must have been caused in it by another. Then it is argued that in addition to any natural causes that are involved, a cause resembling what is commonly called God is necessary. Let's briefly outline this structure in each of the five ways.

The first way begins by trying to account for some kinds of accidental changes we experience through our senses, such as the *person*, who moves a *hand* that moves a *shovel*. Because no being can be (at the same time) in a state of actuality and potentiality with respect to the same thing, this way eventually leads, through a hierarchical causal series, to a first efficient cause that is pure actuality.

The second way focuses on efficient causality in general, arguing that any hierarchical order of efficient causes we encounter demands a first uncaused efficient cause. While similar to the first way, the second way is broader. Thomas says that it is impossible for a thing to be the efficient cause of itself. Therefore, instead of focusing on accidental changes in a substance, as in the first way, the second way can be used to argue for a first cause of substances themselves.

The third way focuses on how efficient causality is related to existence. Substances that are generated, such as Mary, only possess existence contingently, not necessarily. This way eventually concludes that only a being that exists necessarily through itself can explain why anything exists at all.

The fourth way is particularly tricky. It involves exemplar causation, which is related to the formal cause. To understand it, let's return to the example of the statue. The material and formal causes of the statue, the marble and the shape, are intrinsic to the statue. They are part of the actual statue just like eyes and a nose are part of a human being. However, in this case, the efficient cause, the sculptor, is extrinsic to the statue. But isn't it true that the sculptor had in mind what kind of statue he or she wanted to produce before beginning the project? Suppose the sculptor wanted to produce a statue of a three-headed lion. The shape that exists in the sculptor's mind prior to making the statue is called the exemplar cause. It is that in the likeness of which something is made.[117] The sculptor tries to bring the shape of the statue into conformity with the shape in his or her mind (the exemplar cause). For this reason, the exemplar cause is called the extrinsic formal cause. In the fourth way, Aquinas argues that the gradations or degrees of goodness we see among the things of the world indirectly show us that these things only possess being in a limited way. This way eventually argues to a cause that is unlimited or maximal being, which is both the efficient *and* exemplar cause of the being of all things.

Finally, the fifth way focuses on the final causality exhibited by non-intelligent natural things, such as an electron, which has a natural inclination to be attracted to the proton. When studying the fifth way, along with other texts of

Aquinas that help to clarify it, it becomes clear that when something non-intelligent has a natural inclination to act for an end (a goal) that is good, an intelligent cause external to it is needed to explain why it has that natural inclination.

9. Reasoning to God's Existence (And Why God Cannot Be Defined)

The astute reader of this chapter will notice that, strictly speaking, no *definition* of God has been given above. Indeed, even Aquinas himself ends each of the five ways only with a short sentence, expressing something along the lines of "and this we call God." Some would argue that lacking a definition of God invalidates all of the five ways, but this is not so.[118] Earlier in the *Summa theologiae*, Aquinas argued the following: "When the existence of a cause is demonstrated from an effect, this effect takes the place of the definition of the cause in proof of the cause's existence."[119] He goes on to say that the question of essence comes only *after* the question of existence has been settled. Let's clarify this with an example.

Suppose, upon returning to your home after a vacation, you notice that the back door to your house is open. Normally, it is locked. Thomas argues that "from every effect the existence of its cause can be demonstrated."[120] Indeed, doors do not unlock themselves, so there must be a cause for the effect (the open door). At this point, the effect takes the place of the definition of the cause. That is, we are looking for the "door-opener," to put it generically, even though we don't know the essence of the cause. It could be that a human picked the lock. Or perhaps the door was accidently left unlocked and the wind blew it open. However, later, when the hidden safe is found open and empty, it is clear the "door-opener" was an intelligent being.

Similarly, each of the five ways reasons to a cause, such as the Necessary Being, or the Uncaused Cause, etc. When all of the five ways are added together, a cause that is perfect, unchanging, uncaused, intelligent, and necessary being, and which is the cause of the existence of all things, comes into focus. This description, while not a definition, clearly resembles the Creator God of Christianity and some other monotheistic religions.

In the end, if Aquinas is correct that God is Being Itself, then no definition of God is possible. To define something is to break it down into simpler concepts. For example, *human* can be broken down into *rational* and *animal*. But not everything can be defined because then there would be an infinite regress. So, eventually we must come across something that is most foundational in reality and therefore cannot be broken down any further. Being is that which is most foundational in reality; therefore, being—and thus Being Itself, which is God—is indefinable.

Reasoning to God's existence, and the recognition that God is *Existence Itself*, gives us some insight into the great importance of existence in reality and in Aquinas's thought. But, for humans, grasping existence is difficult. Existence is not a color we can see with our eyes; it is not a sound we can hear with our ears. Existence is neither an accidental property of a substance nor a primary substance itself. Accidents and substances *have* existence, but they are not existence.

In the case of physical things, existence is the *act* or *actuality* of a physical thing, but it is not a physical thing itself. Here an analogy might be helpful. Consider a human runner. The *act of running* is not a separate substance from the human runner. But the act of running makes the runner exist in a certain way. Existence is analogous to the act of running, because just as the act of running makes the human runner exist in a certain way, namely as running as opposed to sleeping, so the act of existing makes an essence, for example human, exist as opposed to not existing.

Because in physical things existence is related to essence as actuality to potentiality, there is a real distinction between existence and essence in physical things. And because existence is really distinct from essence, we cannot grasp existence as we would an essence. An essence, for example "human," is properly understood through concepts, namely, rational and animal. But, as we have seen above, existence is indefineable and therefore cannot be understood adequately through concepts, even if we can in our minds have a rough understanding of what it means when we use the word "existence."

Existence, then, is not grasped in sensation or conceptualization, but through a different act of the mind whereby we become aware of things existing before us.[121] Whether it's our awareness of the existence of a friend who has just walked into the room, or the awareness we have of our own existence, our minds can become aware of the existence of the things we encounter. And should we be blessed one day to gaze upon *Existence Itself*, we will grasp, as much as our limited essence can, the perfect truth, goodness, and beauty of the God in whose image we are made.

Chapter 11
Synopses of the Five Ways

The synopses below are *not* a substitute for the preceding chapters, which should be read first. Indeed, the dialogue format was specifically chosen to make the five ways more understandable by explaining the concepts and principles involved, giving multiple examples and analogies, and raising and answering objections along the way. At times, Lucy also updates the five ways to handle new discoveries and objections from the modern sciences. Finally, in chapter seven, she realizes that the five ways must be interpreted in an *existential* way, something that many people miss. However, for those who have read the preceding chapters, we feel that it might also be useful to have short summaries of Lucy's versions of the five ways, which we have provided below.

The First Way

The same property (for example, health) cannot both exist and not exist in the same subject (for example, Lucy) at the same time and in the same way. As such, the same thing cannot be both in actuality with respect to X and in potentiality with respect to X at the same time. We know through observation that things in the world change. If something—let's call it A—is changed, it is reduced from potentiality to actuality by something in a state of actuality. But A cannot actualize its own potentiality because, as is clear from above, the same thing cannot be both in actuality with respect to X and in potentiality with respect to X at the same time. So, if A is changed, it is reduced from potentiality to actuality by something else, B, which is in a state of actuality. But if B was only in a state of actuality because it was changed, then it had to be actualized by another cause, C. But if C was only in a state of actuality because it was changed, then it had to be actualized by another cause, D. We cannot keep going on to infinity if we wish to explain the fact that things change, which we know from observation. This is because in a series of hierarchically (or essentially) ordered causes, none of the causes are in a state of actuality except insofar as they are actualized by a first cause. For example, the stone only moves because the stick moves it, and the stick only moves because the hand moves it, and the hand only moves because the person moves it. If the person does not move the hand, then the stick and the stone will not be in a state of actuality. Thus, in order to explain the change we observe, there must be a first cause, an unmoved mover, which changes other things but which is not itself changed. This can only be true of a cause that is pure actuality (that is, containing no potentiality); and so the unmoved mover must be pure actuality. Now, existence is that which makes every thing actual, for something is actual only if it exists. Therefore, if essence and existence are really distinct in a being, then existence must be compared to essence, as actuality to potentiality. But there is no potentiality in the unmoved mover, only actuality, as was made clear above. Therefore, existence is not distinct from essence, but is rather identical to it, in the unmoved mover. Thus, the unmoved mover must be pure existence (or Being Itself). And this we call God.

The Second Way

In the world of sensible things, we find essentially ordered series of efficient causes—for example, the person who moves his hand, to move a stick, to move a stone. Another example would be a piece of gold, which is efficiently caused by the joining of atoms, which are efficiently caused by the joining of particles (electrons, protons, and neutrons), etc. No thing can be the efficient cause of itself. This is because if it caused itself, then it would be both prior *and* not prior to itself, which is a contradiction and thus impossible. Therefore, if we observe an effect from an essentially ordered series of efficient causes, there must be a first cause that is uncaused. This is because in an essentially ordered series of efficient causes, each cause leading up to the effect is dependent on all of the prior causes. So, if you remove the first cause, then the intermediate causes will have no causal power, and the effect will not be produced. Therefore, an essentially ordered series of efficient causes cannot be infinite because then there will be no first cause and consequently no effect. But we see the effect of an essentially ordered series of efficient causes. Therefore, a first cause must exist, and it must be uncaused; otherwise, it would derive its causal power from another and would be an intermediate cause and not a first cause. Now, if the existence of a thing is really distinct from its essence, then that thing must receive existence from an external cause, because no thing is the cause of its own existence. But the uncaused cause cannot receive its existence from another because then it would be caused and not uncaused. Therefore, existence is not distinct from essence, but is rather identical to it, in the uncaused cause.

Thus, the uncaused cause must be pure existence (or Being Itself). And this we call God.

Third Way

We find in reality some things that are capable of existing and not existing, and we know this because they are found to be generated and to corrupt (for example, human beings are generated by parents and eventually die, passing out of existence). We call such beings "possible beings." A possible being cannot be the cause of its own existence. This is because it would already have to exist in order to cause its own existence, but if it already exists, then it does not need to cause its own existence. Therefore, a possible being must get its existence from a cause that exists external to it. It is impossible that everything which exists is a possible being. This is because a possible being only comes to exist through an already existing cause external to it; but if everything were a possible being, then there'd be no way to explain how anything came into existence in the first place. But if nothing could have begun to exist in reality, then nothing would have existed in the past, and nothing would exist now, because "from nothing, nothing comes." But this is absurd because things exist now. Thus, not all things are possible beings—at least one necessary being must exist. There are two ways for a being to be necessary: (1) it can get its necessity from another, or (2) it can get its necessity from itself (*per se*). If it has its necessity from another, then it requires a cause external to it. Now, it is impossible to go on to infinity in necessary beings which have their necessity caused by another, as has been already proved in the second way with respect to essentially ordered efficient causes. Thus, there must be a first being, which exists necessarily from itself (*per se*) and which causes in other beings their necessity. Now, if the existence of a thing is really distinct from its essence, then that thing must receive existence from an external cause, because no thing is the cause of its own existence. But anything that receives existence from another cannot be that which exists necessarily from itself (*per se*). Therefore, existence is not distinct from essence, but is rather identical to it, in that which exists necessarily from itself. Thus, that which exists necessarily from itself (*per se*) must be pure existence (or Being Itself). And this we call God.

The Fourth Way

Every being we encounter possesses goodness to some degree. This is true because of the following argument. Goodness is related to the level of *perfection* of a being. For the more perfect something is, the more we desire it. And the level of perfection of a being is measured according to the kinds of actions it performs, because perfection is related to actuality. The more actuality (and the less potentiality) a being has, the more powerful kinds of actions it can perform. Now, we know through observation that some kinds of beings are better (possess greater goodness) than others. For example, plants are better than stones because plants are alive, and humans are better than plants because humans are alive and intelligent. To talk about an attribute such as goodness is to indirectly talk about being (existence) because a thing has actuality only if it exists. Everything that exists, therefore, will have some level of actuality, and therefore some level of perfection, and therefore some level of goodness. In contrast, only some kinds of beings possess life or intelligence. Therefore, everything we encounter possesses goodness and being to some degree. But we can only judge that different kinds of things have more or less being to the extent that they resemble or approach (in different ways) something which is maximal being. Now the maximum in any genus is the cause of all in that genus when two conditions are true: (1) when the things in the genus require a cause, and (2) when it's impossible for the cause of the things in the genus to be outside of that genus. Condition two is true because it is impossible for a cause of things in the genus *being* to be outside of the genus *being,* for to "be" outside of the genus of *being* is to be non-being, or nothing, which cannot act as a cause. Condition one is true because of the following argument. If something's essence were identical to its existence, it would be pure existence and also pure actuality, for existence is what makes something actual. Additionally, it would be totally perfect because, as explained above, the level of perfection is related to the level of actuality. But none of the beings we experience in life are totally perfect. This implies that something must be limiting their existence, namely, their essence or nature. Plants cannot walk or reason because their nature limits what they can do. So, when a thing only possesses being in a limited way, such as a plant does, it implies that the thing in question had the potential to receive being but only to a degree. But something cannot actualize its own potential to receive being, for then it would cause its own existence, which is impossible. Therefore, a cause external to it must give it being. And it is for this reason that all things which possess being in a limited way require a cause. Therefore, there must be something which is to all limited beings the cause of their being, goodness, and every other perfection they have. Now, the cause of all these limited beings cannot itself possess being in a limited way—otherwise, it too would require a cause. So, the cause of the being of limited beings must be unlimited or maximal being. Now, if essence and existence are really distinct in a being, then existence must be compared to essence, as actuality to potentiality. But in such a case the essence, as potentiality, limits existence. But this cannot be true of maximal being, since it is not limited in any way. Therefore, existence is not distinct from essence, but is rather identical to it, in maximal being. Thus, the maximal being must be pure existence (or Being Itself). And this we call God.

The Fifth Way

We see in nature that non-intelligent things act for a goal that is good with regularity. For example, it is in the nature of an electron to be attracted to protons, which helps to form atoms. If electrons did not have this natural inclination, then none of the elements on the periodic table you studied in Chemistry would form, which would mean that none of the physical life-forms we know (including yourself) would exist anywhere in the physical universe. If you agree that life, including your own life, is good, then it's hard to see the natural inclination of the electron to the proton as anything other than good. Now, in the case of electrons being attracted to protons, we cannot ascribe such behavior to chance or to biological evolution. In the case of chance, chance would not explain why the electrons act with such regularity because chance refers to what happens rarely. In the case of biological evolution, this is because the regularity of action in the case of electrons exists prior to biological evolution and is necessary for biological evolution to be possible. Now, an intelligent cause can direct something for a goal that is good with regularity. For example, consider an archer who, with routine success, directs his arrows towards a target. An intelligent cause can do this because having intelligence allows one to envision something mentally that does not yet exist physically and choose a means to achieve that end. However, non-intelligent matter, such as a stone or an electron, cannot order itself to an end because it cannot think freely about a future that does not yet exist. Indeed, a stone or an electron does not have knowledge of any kind, and so it is confined to the here and now. So, if an electron has a natural inclination to something outside of itself—the proton—an end it could neither have known about nor have established, then that inclination must have been caused in it by an intelligent cause exterior to it. However, human intelligence cannot account for the *natural* inclinations of things. For example, in the case of the archer, the action of the arrows, which routinely hit the target, do not represent the natural actions of wood, from which the arrows are made. Instead, that end of hitting the target is imposed on the wood of the arrow, which is an example of extrinsic finality. This is because it is not a natural inclination of wood to fly through the air and hit targets. Other examples of extrinsic finality include the puppeteer, who imposes movement on a puppet, and the watchmaker, who orders the metal parts of a watch to do something that's contrary to its nature—to tell time. In our attempt to explain why electrons, as non-intelligent beings, have a natural inclination to be attracted to protons, which makes life possible, we have ruled out: (1) the material aspect of the electron (that is, non-intelligent matter), (2) chance, (3) biological evolution, and (4) any intelligence that uses only extrinsic finality (such as human intelligence). Therefore, there must be some non-human intelligence that is responsible for the natural inclinations of electrons. This non-human intelligence cannot achieve this by extrinsic finality—that is, by imposing activity on the electron in a manner similar to a puppeteer or a watchmaker, because then it would not be a natural inclination. Instead, this non-human intelligence must use intrinsic finality—that is, it must be the cause responsible for the electron's existence and nature, which includes its natural inclinations. Only an intelligent cause that is pure existence (or Being Itself) can cause the existence, nature, and natural inclinations of things. And this we call God.

Five Ways, One God

All of the five ways conclude to a cause that is pure existence (or Being Itself). As argued above, there is no composition of actuality and potentiality, but rather only pure actuality, in Being Itself; and there is no real distinction between existence and essence, but rather only pure existence, in Being Itself. In order for the five ways to support the monotheism of Christianity, we must show two things. First, that there can be only one being that is pure existence, and so only one God; and, second, that Being itself is worthy of being called "God," as that name is used in the Christian tradition.

The first argument is as follows. In order for there to be two beings that are pure existence, one must have a property that the other does not have—otherwise, they would *not* be two different beings, but one and the same being. But if one has a property the other does not have, then it is a composite of existence and *some property*—and not *pure* existence after all. Additionally, a composite being, because it is the union of two really distinct parts, needs a cause to unite these parts. But as argued above, pure existence is uncaused. Therefore, there can only be one being that is pure existence (or Being Itself).

The second argument is that the name "God" is appropriately used of Being Itself because, as the five ways show, Being Itself closely resembles the God of Christianity. The five ways show that Being Itself is: (1) pure actuality (and thus unchanging), (2) uncaused (but the first efficient cause of all other things), (3) that which exists necessarily through itself (and thus the cause of the existence of all other things), (4) maximal being (and thus perfect and that which all other beings resemble in some way), and (5) intelligent (and thus responsible for the order and purpose we find in the universe). St. Thomas goes on to demonstrate other attributes of Being Itself in questions 2-26 of the first part of the *Summa theologiae* (for example, that Being Itself is loving, just, and all-powerful). The result of all of these arguments is a compelling rational case that Being Itself is worthy of the name "God," as used in the Christian tradition.

Chapter 12
Suggested Readings

Here is some further reading material that will assist you in learning more about the arguments for and against the existence of God. We have broken the readings into three categories: beginner, intermediate, and advanced.

Beginner

20 Answers: Atheism, by Matt Fradd

20 Answers: God, by Trent Horn

The Reality of God: The Layman's Guide to Scientific Evidence for the Creator, by Steve Hemler

Who Designed the Designer?, by Michael Augros

Intermediate

An Introduction to the Philosophy of Religion, by Brian Davies

Answering Atheism: How to Make the Case for God with Logic and Charity, by Trent Horn

Aquinas: A Beginner's Guide, by Ed Feser

God Under Fire, edited by Douglas Huffman and Eric Johnson

The Experience of God: Being, Consciousness and Bliss, by David Bentley Hart

The Last Superstition: A Refutation of the New Atheism, by Ed Feser

The Philosophy of Aquinas, second edition, by Robert Pasnau and Christopher Shields

Introduction to the Philosophy of St. Thomas Aquinas, Volume 4: Metaphysics, by H. D. Gardeil

Advanced

God and Moral Obligation, by C. Stephen Evans

New Proofs for the Existence of God: Contributions of Contemporary Physics and Philosophy, by Fr. Robert J. Spitzer

The Blackwell Companion to Natural Theology, edited by William Lane Craig

The Metaphysical Thought of Thomas Aquinas: From Finite Being to Uncreated Being, by John F. Wippel

St. Thomas Aquinas on the Existence of God: The Collected Papers of Joseph Owens, edited by John. R. Catan

An Elementary Christian Metaphysics, by Joseph Owens

St. Thomas and the Future of Metaphysics, by Joseph Owens

A Not-So-Elementary Christian Metaphysics, by Peter A. Redpath

A Not-So-Elementary Christian Metaphysics: Volume Two, by Peter A. Redpath

The Preface to Thomistic Metaphysics, by John F. X. Knasas

Unlocking Divine Action: Contemporary Science and Thomas Aquinas, by Michael J. Dodds, OP

Afterword

Robert A. Delfino

Fr. W. Norris Clarke (1915-2008), a famous scholar of Aquinas, once said:

> It takes about ten years [of study] to get really at home in St.
> Thomas. What we need now is to have some way of stream-
> lining St. Thomas, getting his great seminal ideas and putting
> them across so people can understand them easily, see their rel-
> evance to their lives without having to go through a whole long
> technical training ... That's what I call creative retrieval of the
> thought of St. Thomas ... [But] whenever you re-express the
> thought of an older thinker in your own terms, more modern
> terms, you are taking a risk, but without that the seed can't take
> root in new soil. It is just restricted to a smaller group.[122]

Through the dialogue of AJ and Lucy, Matt and I have tried our best to
explain the five ways of Aquinas in simple and meaningful ways. Of course,
we didn't address every objection that can be raised, and we didn't cover all
of the important things that Aquinas argues about God. But we hope we
have inspired you to continue the dialogue by thinking about the topic of
God, raising new questions, and searching for the best answers. To encour-

age you in this, I'd like to discuss how the thought of Thomas Aquinas can help us understand the sheer immensity of God's love for us and how this sheds light on the meaning of life and existence. In fact, as I shall explain below, the theme of existence is intimately connected to God's love for us.

If you've made it this far, it should be clear just how important *existence* is in the thought of Thomas Aquinas. Indeed, right after the five ways, Aquinas argues that God is Pure Existence or Being Itself (*Ipsum Esse*). In other words, God's existence is not limited by human nature or any other kind of essence. Instead, God's existence and essence are identical. Because only one being can be Existence Itself, in everything else there is a real distinction between existence and essence. To grasp this distinction requires understanding that, in creatures, existence is related to essence as actuality to potentiality. And to explain that, let's consider some of the causes involved in producing a marble statue.

The statue is made out of marble, which is the material cause. But it is the form, or shape of the statue, that tells you whether it is a statue of St. Peter or something else. The marble has the potential to be carved into different shapes, but an uncarved piece of marble is not a statue. It is only after the statue receives its form from the sculptor that it actually is a statue of St. Peter or something else. This means that form is related to matter as actuality to potentiality. Matter has the *potential* to receive form, and once it is received, the form is what *actually* makes it a statue of St. Peter or something else.

For Aquinas, existence is related to essence in a way similar to (analogous to) how form is related to matter. For example, an essence, such as Tyrannosaurus Rex, has the potential to receive existence—but until it actually receives existence, it is nothing. There was a time when dinosaurs had existence, but they exist no longer. They were able to lose their existence precisely because their essence was really distinct from their existence. Only God can never lose His existence because He is Existence Itself.

This means that creatures are only *beings by participation* because they must receive their existence from God. As Aquinas expresses it, "That which *has* existence but *is not* existence, is a being by participation."[123] Therefore, it is only because God gives us existence that we exist at all. But this raises an important question—Why did God create us? Indeed, why did God create anything at all?

The answer is not immediately apparent. Aquinas tells us that God, as Being Itself, is pure actuality—God has no unrealized potential. Indeed, God is perfect—lacking nothing whatsoever. So, it can't be that God created us because God was lonely or because He wanted something from us. And it can't be that God was forced or caused by something else to create us, because Aquinas argues that God is all-powerful and free.[124]

So, why would God create us? It turns out that the answer is *love*. God, being in love with His own Being, wanted to multiply it as much as possible. So, God gave a likeness of His Being to creatures. God couldn't duplicate Himself, so, as Aquinas explains, God created a diversity of things to reflect Him: "In order that the likeness of divine goodness might be more perfectly communicated to things, it was necessary for there to be a diversity of things, so that what could not be perfectly represented by one thing might be, in more perfect fashion, represented by a variety of things in different ways."[125]

So, love is the reason, but not the cause, why God creates.[126] To love someone is to will something good towards that person.[127] And in giving us existence, life, and intelligence, God has given human beings good things—

wondrous things. It is only by having existence that we can enjoy the beauty of a sunset, the company of a friend, the laughter of a young child, and falling in love with another person. Thus, it is only by having existence that we can participate in the goodness of *being*, which is to participate, in our own limited way, in God's wondrous life.

This sheds light on the meaning of human life and existence. Love is the reason for our creation, and we are called to share a life of love with God and other persons. Indeed, we have hearts and minds so we can come to know and freely love one another—and the One who made us. Human happiness cannot be found in money or fame or pleasure or other such things—but only in loving other persons and, ultimately, in loving and being loved by God.[128]

This is the great gift God gives to us. But as I said above, love must be freely given. God does not force us to love Him, or others, or even ourselves. But like the Parable of the Prodigal Son (Lk 15:11-32), God waits for us to return to Him in love. God's love never falters or fails. As pure actuality, God cannot change, and so His love for us never changes. No matter what we do, God loves us and is willing to forgive us. His invitation to us to share life with Him is always open, but it's up to us to respond.

Seminary of the Immaculate Conception

Huntington, NY, 2017

Endnotes

PREFACE

1. First Vatican Council, Dogmatic Constitution *Dei Filius* (24 April 1870), §2.

2. John Paul II, Encyclical on the Relationship between Faith and Reason *Fides et ratio* (14 September 1998).

INTRODUCTION

3. Thomas Aquinas, *Summa theologiae*, I, q. 2, a. 3, in *Summa theologica: Complete English Edition in Five Volumes*, vol. 1, trans. Fathers of the English Dominican Province (Notre Dame, IN: Christian Classics, 1981). Unless noted, all translations of the *Summa theologiae* are taken from this edition. You can find most of Aquinas's works in English and Latin on the website of the Dominican House of Studies (Priory of the Immaculate Conception): http://www.dhspriory.org/thomas/.

4. The most important of these works are *Commentary on the Sentences of Peter Lombard* (*Commentum in Quatuor Libris Sententiarum*), *Summary against the Gentiles* (*Summa contra gentiles*), *Summary of Theology* (*Summa theologiae*), *Disputed Questions concerning the Power of God* (*Quaestiones disputate de potentia Dei*), and *Commentary on the Gospel of St. John* (*Expositio in Evangelium S. Joannis*).

CHAPTER 1: AN ATHEIST AND A CHRISTIAN WALK INTO A COFFEE SHOP

5. Richard Dawkins, *The God Delusion* (Boston: Houghton Mifflin, 2006), 31.

6. William L. Rowe, "Atheism," in *Routledge Encyclopedia of Philosophy*, ed. Tim Crane, at www.rep.routledge.com.

7.   This analogy is from Trent Horn.

8.   Trent Horn, *Answering Atheism: How to Make the Case for God with Logic and Charity* (San Diego: Catholic Answers, 2013), 22.

CHAPTER 2: THE PROBLEM OF EVIL

9.   James R. Beebe, "Logical Problem of Evil," in *The Internet Encyclopedia of Philosophy*, ed. James Fieser and Bradley Dowden, at www.iep.utm.edu.

10. J. L. Mackie, "Evil and Omnipotence," *Mind* 64, no. 254 (1955), 200-212.

11. Thomas Aquinas, *Summa theologiae*, I, q. 25, a. 3, in *Summa theologica: Complete English Edition in Five Volumes*, vol. 1, trans. Fathers of the English Dominican Province (Notre Dame, IN: Christian Classics, 1981).

12. C. S. Lewis, *The Problem of Pain* (New York: HarperOne, 2015), 18.

13. St. Augustine of Hippo, *On Free Choice of the Will*, trans. Thomas Williams (Indianapolis: Hackett, 1993), 81.

14. Lewis, *Problem of Pain*, 31.

15. David Hume, *A Treatise of Human Nature*, III, 1, 1, ed. L. A. Selby-Bigge, 2nd ed. (Oxford: Oxford University Press, 1978), 469.

16. Alasdair MacIntyre, *After Virtue*, 2nd ed. (Notre Dame, IN: University of Notre Dame Press, 1984), 58. See also Robert A. Delfino, "The Failure of New Atheism Morality," *Studia Gilsoniana* 4, no. 3 (2015), 229–240, at http://www.gilsonsociety.com/files/229-240-Delfino.pdf.

17. Richard Dawkins, *River Out of Eden: A Darwinian View of Life* (New York: Basic Books, 1995), 131-133.

CHAPTER 3: IS SCIENCE THE ONLY WAY TO KNOW TRUTH?

18. Karl Popper, *The Logic of Scientific Discovery* (New York: Routledge, 1992), 249.

19. Robert C. Trundle, *Integrated Truth and Existential Phenomenology: A Thomistic Response to Iconic Anti-Realists in Science* (Leiden: Brill Rodopi, 2015), 73-100.

20. Richard Dawkins, *The God Delusion* (Boston: Houghton Mifflin, 2006), 50.

21. "Science is a way of knowing about the natural world. It is limited to explaining the natural world through natural causes. Science can say nothing about the supernatural. Whether God exists or not is a question about which science is neutral." National Academy of Sciences, *Teaching about Evo-*

lution and the Nature of Science (Washington, DC: National Academy Press, 1998), 58.

22. Jay J. Gould, "Impeaching a Self-Appointed Judge," *Scientific American* 267, no. 1 (1992), 118-121.

23. Mikael Stenmark, *Scientism: Science, Ethics and Religion* (Aldershot, UK: Ashgate, 2001), 18-33.

24. Robert A. Delfino, "The Cultural Dangers of Scientism and Common Sense Solutions," *Studia Gilsoniana* 3, supplement (2014), 485–496, at http://www.gilsonsociety.com/files/485-496-Delfino.pdf.

CHAPTER 4: THE FIRST WAY: ARGUMENT FROM MOTION

25. Richard Dawkins, *The God Delusion* (Boston: Houghton Mifflin, 2006), 77.

26. Thomas Aquinas, *Summa theologiae*, I, q. 2, a. 3, in *Summa theologica: Complete English Edition in Five Volumes*, vol. 1, trans. Fathers of the English Dominican Province (Notre Dame, IN: Christian Classics, 1981).

27. *ST*, I, q. 4, a. 1.

28. "The same Holy mother Church holds and teaches that God, the source and end of all things, can be known (*cognosci posse*) with certainty from the consideration of created things, by the natural power of human reason." First Vatican Council, Dogmatic Constitution *Dei Filius* (24 April 1870), §2.

29. Aquinas is clear at the beginning of the *Summa theologiae*, I, q. 1, a. 1: "Even as regards those truths about God which human reason could have discovered, it was necessary that man should be taught by a divine revelation; because the truth about God such as reason could discover, would only be known by a few, and that after a long time, and with the admixture of many errors."

CHAPTER 5: THE SECOND WAY: ARGUMENT FROM EFFICIENT CAUSALITY

30. Thomas Aquinas, *Summa theologiae*, I, q. 2, a. 3, in *Summa theologica: Complete English Edition in Five Volumes*, vol. 1, trans. Fathers of the English Dominican Province (Notre Dame, IN: Christian Classics, 1981).

31. See William Lane Craig, *The Kalām Cosmological Argument* (Eugene, OR: Wipf & Stock, 2000).

32. Thomas Aquinas, *De aeternitate mundi*, trans. Robert T. Miller (1997), at Ford-

ham University, at http://legacy.fordham.edu/halsall/basis/aquinas-eternity.asp. See also *ST*, I, q. 46, a. 2.

33. "In efficient causes it is impossible to proceed to infinity "per se" [hierarchically]—thus, there cannot be an infinite number of causes that are "per se" required for a certain effect; for instance, that a stone be moved by a stick, the stick by the hand, and so on to infinity. But it is not impossible to proceed to infinity "accidentally" [linearly] as regards efficient causes … Hence it is not impossible for a man to be generated by man to infinity; but such a thing would be impossible if the generation of this man depended upon this man, and on an elementary body, and on the sun, and so on to infinity." *ST*, I, q. 46, a. 2, reply to objection 7.

34. "An essentially ordered causal series is asymmetric, irreflexive, and wholly derivative. The subsequent members in such series are not only caused by and ontologically dependent on the preceding members, as in a transitive series, they also serve as causes only insofar as they have been caused by and are effects of all the preceding members. Because these intermediate causes possess causal powers only by deriving them from all the preceding causes, they need a first and nonderivative cause…. If there were only intermediate and derivative causes, then there would be no source from which the causal powers of the intermediate causes could be derived, regardless of whether there were a finite or an infinite number of intermediate causes." Caleb Cohoe, "There Must Be a First: Why Thomas Aquinas Rejects Infinite, Essentially Ordered Causal Series," *British Journal for the History of Philosophy* (2013), 839-840.

35. Joseph Owens, *An Elementary Christian Metaphysics*, reprint ed. (Houston: Center for Thomistic Studies, 1985), 361-362.

CHAPTER 6: THE THIRD WAY: ARGUMENT FROM POSSIBILITY AND NECESSITY

36. Thomas Aquinas, Summa theologiae, I, q. 2, a. 3, in Summa theologica: Complete English Edition in Five Volumes, vol. 1, trans. Fathers of the English Dominican Province (Notre Dame, IN: Christian Classics, 1981).

37. See Lawrence M. Krauss, *A Universe from Nothing: Why There Is Something Rather than Nothing* (New York: Atria Books, 2013).

38. See Krauss, *Universe from Nothing*, 177-180.

39. David Albert, who is a professor of philosophy at Columbia University, and who has a PhD in Theoretical Physics, comes to the same conclusion in his

review of Krauss's book; see David Albert, "On the Origin of Everything: *A Universe from Nothing* by Lawrence M. Krauss," *New York Times*, March 23, 2012, Sunday Book Review, at http://www.nytimes.com/2012/03/25/books/review/a-universe-from-nothing-by-lawrence-m-krauss.html.

40. John F. Wippel (ed), *The Ultimate Why Question: Why Is There Anything at All Rather than Nothing Whatsoever?* Studies in Philosophy and the History of Philosophy, vol. 54 (Washington, DC: Catholic University of America Press, 2011).

41. *ST*, I, q. 2, a. 3.

42. *ST*, I, q. 2., a. 3.

43. Thomas *Aquinas, Summa contra gentiles*, I, 42, 8, trans. Anton C. Pegis (Notre Dame, IN: University of Notre Dame Press, 1975), 160. Translated into English, the title would be *Summary against the gentiles*. There is good evidence it was intended for Christian missionaries in Spain to answer the objections of non-Christians. See Etienne Gilson, *The Christian Philosophy of St. Thomas Aquinas* (Notre Dame, IN: University of Notre Dame Press, 1956), 385-386.

44. *ST*, I, q. 3, a. 7.

CHAPTER 7: THE VALUE OF OBJECTIONS

45. Aristotle, *Metaphysics*, XII, 6-9, in *The Basic Works of Aristotle*, ed. Richard McKeon, trans. W.D. Ross (New York: Random House, 1941), 878.

46. Aristotle, *Metaphysics*, XII, 6, 1071b20, ed. Richard McKeon, trans. W. D. Ross, 878.

47. Aristotle, *Metaphysics*, XII, 7, 1073a3, ed. Richard Mckeon, trans. W. D. Ross, 881.

48. Aristotle, *Metaphysics*, XII, 8, 1073a13-15, ed. Richard McKeon, trans. W. D. Ross, 881.

49. Aristotle, *Metaphysics*, XII, 8, 1074a14-16, ed. Richard McKeon, trans. W. D. Ross, 883.

50. Aquinas followed Aristotle on this point; see Aristotle, *Metaphysics*, XII, 8. See also Thomas Aquinas, *Summa contra gentiles*, III, 82 (Notre Dame, IN: University of Notre Dame Press, 1975). However, Aquinas did *not* believe the planet Earth was flat: "For the astronomer and the physicist both may prove the same conclusion: that the earth, for instance, is round." Thomas Aquinas, *Summa theologiae*, I, q. 1, a. 1, reply to objection 2, in *Summa theologica: Complete*

English Edition in Five Volumes, vol. 1, trans. Fathers of the English Dominican Province (Notre Dame, IN: Christian Classics, 1981).

51. Joseph Owens, "Aristotle and Aquinas," in *The Cambridge Companion to Aquinas*, ed. Norman Kretzmann and Eleonore Stump (Cambridge, UK: Cambridge University Press, 1993), 38-59.

52. Joseph Owens, "Aquinas and the Five Ways," in *St. Thomas Aquinas on the Existence of God: Collected Papers of Joseph Owens*, ed. John R. Catan (Albany: State University of New York, 1980), 132-141.

53. In Aristotle, *Metaphysics*, VIII, 7, Aristotle says, "When I speak of substance without matter I mean the essence." For Aristotle to say that substance without matter is the essence is for him to identify essence with form alone. Additionally, Aristotle is clear that the unmoved movers are pure form with no matter.

54. "This nature apprehended by the intellect has the character of a universal from its relation to things outside the soul, because it is one likeness of them all ... [Similarly,] if there were a material statue representing many men, the image or likeness of the statue would have its own individual being as it existed in this determinate matter, but it would have the nature of something common as the general representation of many men." Thomas Aquinas, *On Being and Essence*, trans. Armand Maurer, 2nd rev. ed. (Toronto: Pontifical Institute of Mediaeval Studies, 1968), 48-49.

55. *ST*, I, q. 3, a. 4.

56. Joseph Owens, "The Starting Point of the Prima Via," in *St. Thomas Aquinas on the Existence of God: Collected Papers of Joseph Owens*, ed. John R. Catan (Albany: State University of New York, 1980), 169-191. On pages 174-178, Owens explains that the five ways begin with our natural knowledge that the things we experience *exist*. Only after the arguments of the five ways are made does it become clear that there is a real distinction between existence and essence in creatures but not in God.

57. Joseph Owens, *Aristotle's Gradations of Being in Metaphysics E-Z*, ed. Lloyd P. Gerson (South Bend, IN: St. Augustine's Press, 2007), 25-28.

58. *ST*, I, q. 3, a. 4.

CHAPTER 8: THE FOURTH WAY: ARGUMENT FROM DEGREES OF BEING

59. Thomas Aquinas, *Summa theologiae*, I, q. 2, a. 3, in *Summa theologica: Complete*

English Edition in Five Volumes, vol. 1, trans. Fathers of the English Dominican Province (Notre Dame, IN: Christian Classics, 1981).

60. John F. X. Knasas, *The Preface to Thomistic Metaphysics* (New York: Peter Lang, 1990), 126-128. See also Leonard Boyle, *The Setting of the "Summa theologiae" of Saint Thomas* (Toronto: Pontifical Institute of Mediaeval Studies, 1982), 18; and James A. Weisheipl, *Friar Thomas D'Aquino His Life, Thought and Work* (New York: Doubleday, 1974), 197, 217-218.

61. Thomas Aquinas, *De Veritate*, q. 1, a. 2, reply to objection 1, in *Truth*, vol. 3, trans. Robert W. Schmidt (Indianapolis, IN: Hackett, 1994). *De Veritate* translates to *On Truth*.

62. *ST*, I, q. 87, a. 1.

63. *ST*, I, q. 49, a. 1.

64. *ST*, I, q. 4, a. 2, reply to objection 3.

65. *ST*, I, q. 5, a. 1.

66. *ST*, I, q. 2, a. 3.

67. *ST*, I, q. 2, a. 3.

68. *ST*, I, 3, a. 5, in Thomas Aquinas, *The Treatise on the Divine Nature, Summa theologiae I, 1-13*, translated with commentary by Brian Shanley (Indianapolis, IN: Hackett, 2006), 32-33.

69. "Genus can be taken in two ways. One way, properly speaking, as it is predicated of many things, expressing what kind of thing they are. In this way neither good nor bad are genera because they belong to the transcendentals, since good and being are convertible. In another way, generally speaking, so that everything that encompasses and contains many things by its commonness is called a genus. Thus good and bad are called the genera of all contraries." Thomas Aquinas, *Commentary on the Sentences of Peter Lombard*, 2, d. 34, q. 1, a. 2, reply to objection 1 (Robert Delfino's translation).

70. *ST*, I, q. 2, a. 3.

71. Richard Dawkins, *The God Delusion* (Boston: Houghton Mifflin, 2006), 79.

72. Michael Augros, "Twelve Questions About the 'Fourth Way,'" *Aquinas Review* 12 (2005), 1-35.

73. *ST*, I, q. 2, a. 3.

74. Augros, "Twelve Questions About the 'Fourth Way,'" 24.

75. "Whatever a thing possesses by its own nature, and not from some other cause, cannot be diminished and deficient in it....Therefore, whatever belongs to one thing less than to others belongs to it not by virtue of its own nature alone, but through some other cause. Thus, that thing of which a genus is chiefly predicated will be the cause of everything in that genus. So we see that what is most hot is the cause of heat in all hot things; and what is most light, the cause of all illuminated things. But as we proved in Book I, God is being in the highest mode. Therefore, He is the cause of all things of which being is predicated." Thomas Aquinas, *Summa contra gentiles*, II,15, 3, trans. James F. Anderson (Notre Dame, IN: University of Notre Dame Press, 1975), 47.

76. *ST*, I, q. 2, a. 2, reply to objection 3.

77. *ST*, I, q. 4, a. 2.

78. In *ST*, I, q. 13, Aquinas argues that words like "wise" and "being" neither have the same meaning nor mean completely different things when applied to God and humans. Instead, "wise" and "being" are only said of God *analogously*. Analogy is one of the most important keys to unlock the thought of Aquinas. For more information on Thomas's teaching on analogy, see Peter A. Redpath, *A Not-So-Elementary Christian Metaphysics: Volume Two* (St. Louis, MO: En Route Books & Media, 2016), 47-56.

79. Exodus 3:14, Knox Translation. Of course, Aquinas would have read this verse in Latin, not English or Hebrew. And in Latin, Exodus 3:14 reads as follows: *"Dixit Deus ad Moysen: Ego sum qui sum. Ait: Sic dices filiis Israël: Qui est, misit me ad vos."* Now, *"Ego sum qui sum"* translates to "I Am Who Am." And *"Qui est"* translates to "He Who Is." Aquinas, and others in the history of the Church, have interpreted these phrases as signifying that God is Being Itself. For a summary of the Roman Catholic interpretation of Exodus 3:14 from Patristic times to the present day, see Ludwig Ott, *Fundamentals of Catholic Dogma*, ed. James Canon Bastible, trans. Patrick Lynch, 4th ed. (Rockford, IL: TAN Books and Publishers, 2009), 25-27.

CHAPTER 9: THE FIFTH WAY: ARGUMENT FROM FINALITY

80. Thomas Aquinas, *Summa theologiae*, I, q. 2, a. 3, in *Summa theologica: Complete English Edition in Five Volumes*, vol. 1, trans. Fathers of the English Dominican Province (Notre Dame, IN: Christian Classics, 1981). The translation by the Fathers of the English Dominican Province has been modified.

81. Richard Dawkins, *The God Delusion* (Boston: Houghton Mifflin, 2006), 79, 157-158.

82. "Some inclination follows every form: for example, fire, by its form, is inclined to rise, and to generate its like." *ST*, I, q. 80, a. 1. "Natural appetite is nothing but an inclination and ordination of the thing to something else which is in keeping with it, like the ordination of a stone to a place below." Thomas Aquinas, *De Veritate*, q. 25, a. 1, in *Truth*, vol. 3, trans. Robert W. Schmidt (Indianapolis, IN: Hackett, 1994), 213.

83. "Every agent [whether intelligent or not], of necessity, acts for an end. For if, in a number of causes ordained to one another, the first be removed, the others must, of necessity, be removed also. Now the first of all causes is the final cause. The reason of which is that matter does not receive form, save in so far as it is moved by an agent; for nothing reduces itself from potentiality to act. But an agent does not move except out of intention for an end (*ex intentione finis*). For if the agent were not determinate to some particular effect, it would not do one thing rather than another: consequently in order that it produce a determinate effect, it must, of necessity, be determined to some certain one, which has the nature of an end. And just as this determination is effected, in the rational nature, by the 'rational appetite,' which is called the will; so, in other [non-intelligent] things, it is caused by their natural inclination (*per inclinationem naturalem*), which is called the 'natural appetite.'" *ST*, I-II, q, 1, a. 2. Also, "Further, upon the form follows an inclination to the end (*inclinatio ad finem*), or to an action, or something of the sort; for everything, in so far as it is in act, acts and tends (*tendit*) towards that which is in accordance with its form." *ST*, I, q, 5, a. 5.

84. "One could … [postulate] that some external agent intervenes directly from outside each time to bring about the same good result for the natural body. But St. Thomas clearly would not consider this an intelligible alternative, and quite rightly so. For in this case, one would have no right to say that the action was that of the natural body itself, i.e., proceeding from its own nature as center of action. But this would cancel out the very data from which we began: the activity of non-cognitive natural bodies, as natural agents. Hence this phase of the argument concludes that the only sufficient explanation for the regular activity of non-cognitive natural bodies is some built-in intrinsic orientation of their natures, as agents, toward their proper ends. This is final causality, i.e., an intrinsic intentio finis or ontological dynamism of tending toward an end appropriate to the nature of the agent. And this end, like all ends, has the character of the good for the agent tending to it." Leszek Figurski, *Finality and Intelligence: Is the Universe Designed?* (Wydawnictwo Bezkresy Wiedzy, 2014), 142.

85. Dawkins, *God Delusion*, 79.

86. *ST*, I-II, q. 1, a. 2; our emphasis. The translation by the Fathers of the English Dominican Province has been modified.

87. Figurski, *Finality and Intelligence*, 85-88, 145.

88. Fr. W. Norris Clarke gives a similar adaptation of the fifth way, noting, "The ordering of the natural properties of these elements [in the Cosmos] towards dynamic interaction must be constituted prior (priority of causal dependence, not necessarily temporal priority) to their actual operations of interacting, since they interact according to their (already constituted) natures. But this means that they must be ordered toward, constituted in view of, not yet existing future actions, or possible future actions. Now, only a mind can constitute out of possibility a future order, can 'order means to an end,' as St. Thomas likes to put it. Only a mind can thus make present in its field of consciousness the future and the possible, which do not exist in themselves and can have only a mental presence. A purely material being without consciousness is locked into the here and now of its place in space and time. To order possibilities with a view to future action is again almost a definition of mind, or certainly one of its most characteristic functions. Thus the cosmos-wide dynamic order of our world system necessarily requires a cosmos-ordering Mind to constitute its order." W. Norris Clarke, "Is Natural Theology Still Viable Today?," in *Explorations in Metaphysics: Being, God, Person* (Notre Dame, IN: University of Notre Dame Press, 1994), 174-175.

89. William Paley, *Natural Theology: Or, Evidences of the Existence and Attributes of the Deity, Collected from the Appearances of Nature*, 6th ed. (New York: Cambridge University Press, 2009).

90. Edward Feser, "Teleology: A Shopper's Guide," *Philosophia Christi* 12, no. 1 (2010),142-159.

91. Paley, *Natural Theology*, 1-2, 19-22.

92. "I contend, therefore, that there is mechanism in animals; that this mechanism is as properly such, as it is in machines made by art." Paley, *Natural Theology*, 88.

93. *ST*, I, q. 103, a.1, reply to objection 3.

94. "The same effect is not attributed to a natural cause and to divine power in such a way that it is partly done by God, and partly by the natural agent; rather, it is wholly done by both, according to a different way." Thomas Aquinas, *Summa contra gentiles*, III, 70, 8, trans. Vernon J. Bourke (Notre Dame, IN: University of Notre Dame Press, 1975), 237. See *Disputed Questions concerning the Power of God*, q. 5, a. 1, for Thomas's argument that God continually sustains

all things in existence, and if God were to cease sustaining them, then they would instantly become nothing (annihilation).

95. "Creation is not change, except according to a mode of understanding. For change means that the same something should be different now from what it was previously. Sometimes, indeed, the same actual thing is different now from what it was before, as in motion according to quantity, quality and place; but sometimes it is the same being only in potentiality, as in substantial change, the subject of which is matter. But in creation, by which the whole substance of a thing is produced, the same thing can be taken as different now and before only according to our way of understanding, so that a thing is understood as first not existing at all, and afterwards as existing." *ST*, I, q. 45, a. 2, reply to objection 2. See also *ST*, I, q. 44-49, and Aquinas, *Summa contra gentiles*, II, 15-21.

96. "This is not a result of the inadequacy of divine power, but of the immensity of His goodness, whereby He has willed to communicate His likeness to things, not only so that they might exist, but also that they might be causes for other things." Aquinas, *Summa contra gentiles*, III, 70, 7, trans. Vernon J. Bourke, 237.

97. Michael Behe, *Darwin's Black Box* (New York: Free Press, 2006), 39.

98. Marie I. George, "Where Intelligent Design and Dawkins Meet," at Mercatornet (3 March 2009), at http://www.mercatornet.com.

CHAPTER 10: PHILOSOPHICAL TERMS AND CONCEPTS

99. An earlier version of the material contained in this chapter was originally published as an ebook titled *You Can Understand Aquinas: A Guide to Thomas' Metaphysical Jargon*, written by Matt Fradd and Robert A. Delfino.

100. Thomas Aquinas, *On Being and Essence*, trans. Armand Maurer, 2nd rev. ed. (Toronto: Pontifical Institute of Mediaeval Studies, 1968), 30-32.

101. "Since being is not a genus, then being cannot be of itself the essence of either substance or accident. Consequently, the definition of substance is not—'a being of itself without a subject,' nor is the definition of accident—'a being in a subject'; but it belongs to the quiddity or essence of substance 'to have existence not in a subject'; while it belongs to the quiddity or essence of accident 'to have existence in a subject.'" Thomas Aquinas, *Summa theologiae*, III, q. 77, a. 1, reply to objection 2, in *Summa theologica: Complete English Edition in Five Volumes*, vol. 1, trans. Fathers of the English Dominican Province (Notre Dame, IN: Christian Classics, 1981).

102. "A substance is a thing to which it belongs to be not in a subject. The name thing takes its origin from the quiddity [the essence], just as the name being comes from to be [to exist]. In this way, the definition of substance is understood as that which has a quiddity to which it belongs to be not in another. Now, this is not appropriate to God, for He has no quiddity save His being. In no way, then, is God in the genus of substance." Thomas Aquinas, *Summa contra gentiles,* I, 25, 10, trans. Anton C. Pegis (Notre Dame, IN: University of Notre Dame Press, 1975), 128.

103. "The word substance signifies not only what exists of itself ... but, it also signifies an essence that has the property of existing in this way—namely, of existing of itself; this existence, however, is not its essence." *ST,* I, q. 3, a. 5, reply to objection 1.

104. *ST,* I, q. 3, a. 4.

105. He expresses this by saying, "It is impossible that in God His existence should differ from His essence." *ST,* I, q. 3, a. 4.

106. *ST,* I, q. 4, a. 2, and q. 11, a. 4.

107. John Matson, "Fact or Fiction? Lead Can Be Turned into Gold: Particle Accelerators Make Possible the Ancient Alchemist's Dream—but at a Steep Cost," *Scientific American* (2014), at https://www.scientificamerican.com/article/fact-or-fiction-lead-can-be-turned-into-gold/.

108. *ST,* I, q. 2, a. 3.

109. *ST,* I, q. 3, a. 4.

110. Aristotle, *Physics,* II, 3, in *The Basic Works of Aristotle,* ed. Richard McKeon, trans. W.D. Ross (New York: Random House, 1941); Aristotle, *Metaphysics,* V, 2, in *The Basic Works of Aristotle,* ed. Richard McKeon, trans. W.D. Ross (New York: Random House, 1941).

111. Aristotle, *Physics,* II; Aristotle, *Metaphysics,* V, 4.

112. Aristotle, *On the Soul,* II, in *The Basic Works of Aristotle,* ed. Richard McKeon, trans. W.D. Ross (New York: Random House, 1941).

113. Aquinas, *On Being and Essence,* 34-36.

114. This is Aristotle's doctrine of hylomorphism; see Aristotle, *On the Soul,* II.

115. Thomas Aquinas, *Commentary on Aristotle's "Physics,"* Book II, Lecture 5, 180, trans. Richard J. Blackwell, Richard J. Spath, and W. Edmund Thirlkel (Notre Dame, IN: Dumb Ox Books, 1999), 95.

116. Aristotle, *Physics*, II, 3.

117. *ST*, I, q. 35, a. 1, reply to objection 1.

118. For a good article on this, see Victor White, "Prelude to the Five Ways," in *Aquinas's "Summa theologiae": Critical Essays*, ed. Brian Davies (New York: Rowman & Littlefield, 2006), 25-44, especially 40-43.

119. *ST*, I, q. 2, a. 2, reply to objection 2.

120. *ST*, I, q. 2, a. 2.

121. Aquinas explains: "The intellect has two operations: one called the 'understanding of indivisibles,' by which it knows what a thing is, and another by which it joins and divides, that is to say, by forming affirmative and negative statements. Now these two operations correspond to two principles in things. The first operation concerns the nature [or essence] itself of a thing, in virtue of which the object known holds a certain rank among beings, whether it be a complete thing, like some whole, or an incomplete thing, like a part or an accident. The second operation has to do with a thing's [act of existing or] being (*esse*), which results from the union of the principles of a thing in composite substances, or, as in the case of simple substances, accompanies the thing's simple nature." Thomas Aquinas, *Super Boetium De Trinitate*, q. 5, a. 3, trans. Armand A. Maurer, in *The Division and Methods of the Sciences*, 4th ed. (Toronto: Pontifical Institute of Mediaeval Studies, 1986), 34-35. It is now common for Thomists to use the word "judgment" to refer to the second operation of the intellect.

AFTERWORD

122. Fr. W. Norris Clarke made these remarks in an interview that you can watch here: https://www.youtube.com/watch?v=oMt6juNMijk&feature=youtu.be&t=1306. A Transcript is available here: http://www.innerexplorations.com/catchmeta/a1.htm.

123. Thomas Aquinas, *Summa theologiae*, I, q. 3, a. 4, in *Summa theologica: Complete English Edition in Five Volumes*, vol. 1, trans. Fathers of the English Dominican Province (Notre Dame, IN: Christian Classics, 1981); my emphasis.

124. See *ST*, I, q. 25, a. 3, for a defense of God's omnipotence, and *ST*, I, q. 19, a. 10, for a defense of God's freedom.

125. Thomas Aquinas, *Summa contra gentiles*, III, 97, 2, trans. Vernon J. Bourke (Notre Dame, IN: University of Notre Dame Press, 1975), 66.

126. For Thomas's distinction between reason and cause, see Aquinas, *Summa contra gentiles*, I, 86 and 87. See also John F. Wippel, "Thomas Aquinas on the

Ultimate Why Question: Why Is There Anything at All Rather than Nothing Whatsoever?," in *The Ultimate Why Question: Why Is There Anything at All Rather than Nothing Whatsoever?*, ed. John F. Wippel (Washington, DC: Catholic University of America Press, 2011), 84-106, especially 100-104.

127. *ST*, I, q. 20, a. 2.

128. See *ST*, I-II, q. 2, arts 1-8 for those things in which human happiness does not consist; and see *ST*, I-II, q. 3, a. 8, where Aquinas argues that final and perfect human happiness can only consist in union with God in Heaven.

CPSIA information can be obtained
at www.ICGtesting.com
Printed in the USA
LVHW031103170119
604201LV00008B/15/P